LORD PALMERSTON

Anthony Trollope

Pharos Books

ISBN: 978-93-59834-57-3
eISBN: 978-93-59832-67-8

Publisher: Pharos Books (P) Ltd.
Plot No.-63, First Floor, Main Mother Dairy Road
Pandav Nagar, East Delhi-110092
Phone: +14049995474, 011-40395855
WhatsApp: +91 9319228272
E-mail: sales@pharosbooks.in
Website: www.pharosbooks.in
Edition: 2025

Printed By: Sushma Book Binding House, Okhla Industrial Area, Phase II, New Delhi-110020

Lord Palmerston
By : Anthony Trollope

Contents

CHAPTER I
Introduction

IN looking for material on which to base this short memoir of Lord Palmerston I have of course taken, as my guide to his general life, the biography of Mr. Evelyn Ashley.[A] I have also referred to the unfinished volumes by Lord Dalling, which Mr. Ashley adopted as far as they went, and by his later edition has rendered unnecessary to the general reader. Beyond this I have had recourse to the *Edinburgh*, the *Quarterly*, the *Times* newspaper, and various periodicals of the period; and I have read many of his speeches and others. In dealing with the Crimean War I have had recourse to Mr. Kinglake's work; and in various portions of my little book I have referred to other authors, whom it may perhaps be unnecessary that I should name here. Having lived through a great portion of Lord Palmerston's career, I have trusted in some things to my recollection, when I have been able to confirm my memory. But I must add to this short list "The Life of the Prince Consort," by Sir Theodore Martin, in which the name of Lord Palmerston has been brought under much discussion.

Sir Theodore Martin, in that work, has performed a most difficult task with a devotion and loyalty beyond praise. There was a special merit in selecting a man who has united so true a spirit with a patience so exemplary and literary merit of such high character. And the subject of his eulogy was certainly beyond all praise. To have found genius and conscience and industry, with assured moral convictions and a tender loving heart, to fill such a place as that occupied by the Prince Consort, has been the good fortune of England. Let men consider what might have been the condition of the country with a Consort less gifted in any of these details than was the Prince. But with the verdict of the Prince, declared in regard to Lord Palmerston as Foreign Minister, I am compelled to differ. It is nothing that I and another do not agree with it, but I think that I shall be able to show that England has disagreed with his Royal Highness, and that England has been right.

It is better perhaps to say what must be said on this subject here, in the first pages. It has to be said, or such a memoir as this would lack every element of completeness. No man could thoughtfully undertake such a task without feeling that he would have to express an opinion that the Prince was right or wrong. The Prince has been so plain-spoken, and Sir Theodore Martin has been bound to publish what the Prince has said in language so resonant, that no one now dealing with Lord Palmerston's life can pass it over in silence.

That the Prince was conscientious, high-minded, modest in listening to the advice of others, bold in declaring his opinion when he had formed it, and patriotic in declaring it when formed, no thinking man can doubt. Fault was found with him at first, by men who did not think; but that has passed by. It did not now need his "Life" to make his memory sweet to all Englishmen. He came among us and gave us his best, and lived as though we were his own. In pursuance of a theory of government which it was natural that he should adopt, he found fault with the Minister who, at that time, had especially dealt between us and other nations for a period of nearly twenty years. In this he followed the political teaching which he had received from Baron Stockmar, a German possessed of great abilities and gifted with a clear, conscientious mind. He had been left to the Prince as a legacy by his uncle, King Leopold. It can hardly be necessary to speak more in detail of Baron Stockmar after the life of the Prince Consort by Sir Theodore Martin. Lord Palmerston had gone to the Foreign Office in November, 1830, and was dismissed in December, 1851. He had been out of office during six years of that time, and, as we all understand in regard to politicians in opposition, had then watched as closely as he had worked in office. He knew the ways of the Foreign Office. He knew the ways of the Crown. He knew the ways of the people on whose behalf he was employed, and doubtless had a tendency to lessen the power of the Crown rather than to increase it, and to think more of the House of Commons year by year as years ran on. It was only natural that with the Prince the tendencies should be on the other side.

Writing on 19th of December, 1851, Lord John Russell, who was then Prime Minister, said to Lord Palmerston:—"No other course is open to me than to submit the correspondence to the Queen, and to ask her Majesty to appoint a successor to you in the Foreign Office." Thus did Lord John Russell dismiss Lord Palmerston. The Prince, in writing to Lord John, declared that the influence of England in calming down the dangerous feelings on the Continent had been destroyed by Lord Palmerston: "This influence has been rendered null by Lord Palmerston's personal manner of conducting the foreign affairs, and by the universal hatred which he has excited on the Continent. That you could hope to control him has long been doubted by us, and its impossibility is clearly proved by the last proceedings."[B]

No doubt Lord Palmerston had been rough. A man who will not be bullied will sometimes bully. The passage is only quoted here to show the disapproval of Lord Palmerston which existed in the mind of the Prince, and to show also how impossible it will be, in dealing with the life of Palmerston, altogether to ignore the disapproval of the Prince Consort.

The two charges brought against Lord Palmerston were, that by his personal manner of conducting foreign affairs he had "rendered null the influence" of England abroad, and that he had disobeyed the orders received by him from the Court, through the Prime Minister. These orders required that time should be allowed for the reading of despatches prepared by him to be sent to Foreign Courts, and for the making of such alterations as might seem good to the Prime Minister or to the Court. That Lord Palmerston had "rendered null" the influence of England abroad will hardly now be conceived. It will be for me to assert, as Mr. Ashley has well shown, that no Minister has ever more thoroughly supported English interests and English influence abroad. As to a certain amount of disobedience, the disobedience of which complaint is made—I think that it must be admitted. "There," said the head of a Government office one day, when he had just completed the writing of a set of minute instructions to his subordinates—"if they can do all that, I'll eat them." The subordinates by no means intended to be eaten; nor did Lord Palmerston. In all ranks of life there are instructions which a man must not say that he will not obey, but will know that he cannot. So it was with Lord Palmerston. He did not, we suppose, intend to obey those instructions to the letter. He had instructions also from his other master, which made it impossible. He did intend to act as Foreign Minister to the best of his loyalty, and to the best of his patriotism.

For the truth of what is here said, I must refer the reader to the records of the man's life, as about to be given;—as, indeed, they have been given to the same effect, but at much greater length, by Mr. Ashley. Lord Palmerston proved the unassailable strength of his position by the rapidity with which he vanquished his old friend, Lord John, who had dismissed him. How far this dismissal had been carried out by Lord John himself, and how far he had been urged on by the Prince and the Prince's foreign adviser, it is not necessary that I should say. The blow had come from the hands of Lord John, and Lord Palmerston at once hit back at him. On the 19th of December, 1851, he was told to go. On the 24th of February, 1852, he thus wrote to his brother: "I have had my tit for tat with John Russell, and I turned him out on Friday last."

Two months had done it. And how had it been done? Lord Palmerston had found himself called upon to fight the Prime Minister,—and the Ministers who remained in the Cabinet from which he had been dismissed,—backed by all the powers of the Crown. And certainly he could depend in no degree on the House of Lords. It was by the House of Commons,—by his own influence there as opposed to that of Lord John Russell so supported,—that he won his victory. Having won it, he (Lord John) was at once deposed. This, at any rate, showed what was the opinion of those to whom England had confided the political power of the country. The mode of the battle and the cause which created it, must be told further on. It soon became evident that Lord Palmerston had not been "smashed," as had been declared during those months. "There was a Palmerston," had been said by a witty statesman of the opposite party. But it came to pass very soon that Lord Palmerston stood higher than ever in the councils of his country. The war, of which many men said that it would annihilate us, had come upon us; and in four years' time the various Prime Ministers of the day,—Lord Aberdeen and Lord John and Lord Derby,—were calling for help to the "Palmerston that was." Indeed, he had been one of the Cabinet again since December, 1852; and then in February, 1855, himself became Prime Minister, as being the only man in England to whom England could trust the awful responsibility of that period. That was the man on whose dismissal from his councils the Prince had congratulated the then Prime Minister, telling him that England's influence was rendered null by the hatred abroad which the dismissed one had created. This, I think, is strong proof that England did not agree with him. Nor was the Sovereign slow to express her approval of the man who had been so lately dismissed. "It would give her particular satisfaction if Lord Palmerston would join in this formation,"[C]—the formation of a new Cabinet. Then he was called on himself to form a Cabinet, and we are told, in a page or two further on, that "Lord Palmerston had good reason to appreciate the generosity with which his old chief had interposed to remove this formidable impediment to his success. Nor was her Majesty less grateful." So was he welcomed back to the highest seat. Nor was the Prince slow to show himself alive to the fact that the country was best served by him whom the country had selected for its servant. But he must surely then have acknowledged to himself that the dismissal of a Minister of whom England thoroughly approves, though it may be effected for a few months, can hardly be maintained.

This, I think,—his dismissal from the Foreign Office which he loved so well,—was the hardest trial to which Lord Palmerston was subjected during his long official life. In the previous year an attack had been made upon him in regard to Don Pacifico. It had been commenced in the House of Lords, and was carried on through a memorable debate in the House of Commons. During that period the Prince Consort had then written to Lord John:[D] "Both the Queen and myself are *exceedingly sorry* at the news your letter contained. We are not surprised, however, that Lord Palmerston's mode of doing business should not be borne by the susceptible French Government with the same good-humour and forbearance as by his colleagues." But in that affair Lord Palmerston had so managed that he had come out of it, not dismissed, but triumphant. In that, as will be seen, there was no grief to him, though much trouble. But it had all been a part of the same conscientious but, to the feeling of many, unconstitutional operation. It was written on Lord Palmerston's mind that he was England's Minister for Foreign Affairs, acting, no doubt, in conjunction with his colleagues, but subject to no immediate control. But it was not so written on the mind of the Prince Consort. Which idea was written on the minds of the people; and which theory was it possible that either should carry out in accordance with the practice of the country? Subsequently, when Lord Clarendon was Foreign Minister with his entire approval, if not by his nomination, Palmerston must surely have felt more interested in the Foreign Office than any other Englishman. He was greatly successful afterwards as Premier, but his years spent at the Foreign Office were those of his best activity. It is as Foreign Minister that his memory will chiefly live.

He was in office altogether forty-nine years and some odd months;—all but fifty years! No other Englishman has, I believe, ever served so long. How should an Englishman serve so long, seeing that a young man has to show some fitness before he is taken into office, and that then, as parties are divided in England, he has to remain out during that portion of his life in which his opponents are in? But this man did so. He lived in all eighty-one years. Of these, twenty-two were those of his boyhood and education; he enjoyed nine of enforced rest, though during those nine he was, with the exception of a month or two, an active member of Parliament; the remaining fifty saw him always in Parliament, always in office, always at the oar. They offered to make him Lord-Lieutenant of Ireland, as they had also offered to make him Governor-General of India. But he laughed at the proposal. Not to be in the centre of everything,—at St. Stephen's, in Downing Street, in London where the Mayor and the Fishmongers held their banquets, ready for Greenwich dinners, ready for all attacks, for all explanations, for all discussions—was to him not to live. But he did live always, till at eighty-one he was taken to his rest, being at the moment Prime Minister of England.

And yet he was by no means a man of genius, possessed of not more than ordinary gifts of talent, with no startling oratory, and, above all, with no specially strong liberal opinions. He had all that could be done for him, both for good and evil, by a thoroughly English education of the first class. He could fight and would fight as long as he could stand; but as conqueror he could be thoroughly generous. He could work, requiring no rest, but only some change of employment. He shot, he hunted, he raced, he danced. But he seems to have cared for the niceties of erudition neither in classics nor in philosophy. He was a man who from the first was determined to do the best he could with himself; and he did it with a healthy energy, never despairing, never expecting too much, never being in a hurry, but always ready to seize the good thing when it came. Through his active life he was fortunate in all things. He avoided those scrapes to which such men are subject,—men who come early into their fortunes and their titles, who profess to live, if not lives of pleasure, lives to which pleasure lends all her attractions. He shot, he hunted, he raced, and he danced; but he did not drink; he did not gamble. The world has heard of no trouble into which he got about women. He became so popular with the world generally that the world was afraid to be censorious or to inquire into him with prying eyes. The world called him "Cupid" when he was young, and the world said nothing of him more severe than that. He had, too, the great gift of uninterrupted physical health, without which no statesman can now do great things in England. Even a Pitt, were a Pitt to come now, would hardly succeed under the weight of responsibility and labour which he would have to bear.

Lord Palmerston began life as a Tory, and only drifted gradually into those Whig tendencies which held him to the end of his life, rather than were held by him. Of the Honourable Henry John Temple, the eldest son of the Viscount Palmerston of that day, the earliest news we have is that he was measured for his first pair of breeches on the 4th of March, 1789, and that later in life complaints were made that Harry Temple was too sedate and wanted animal spirits;[E] and we know that he passed through Harrow School with fair credit and much popularity as a young nobleman. From thence he was sent to Edinburgh to listen to the teaching of Professor Dugald Stewart. The Professor thus writes about him to his old Harrow master in April, 1801. He was then sixteen. "In point of temper and conduct he is everything his friends could wish. Indeed, I cannot say that I have ever seen a more faultless character at his time of life, or one possessed of a more amiable disposition." It is somewhat exaggerated praise, and would hardly have been believed by Baron Stockmar when, fifty years later on, he had to judge of the Foreign Minister. From Edinburgh he went to St John's, Cambridge. His father had previously died; and here, though we only know it from himself, he was so "commended for the general regularity of his conduct" that he was advised to stand for the University. In January, 1806, Mr. Pitt died, and the University had to elect a new member. Palmerston was twenty-one years old, and was put forward as representing the Tory Government party; but he was beaten by Lord Henry Petty and Lord Althorp, afterwards Lord Lansdowne and Lord Spencer, with both of whom he for many years sat in the same Cabinet. He then stood for Horsham in November, 1806, and was returned; but he was unseated on petition. He stood again for the University, in May, 1807, and was again unsuccessful. He came in afterwards for a rotten borough, Newtown, in the Isle of Wight. "One condition required" by the patron "was that he would never, even for the election, set a foot in the place."

But he had become the officer of the Government before he was a member of Parliament, having, in anticipation of his lot in life, been appointed one of the junior Lords of the Admiralty. He was nominated to that office by the influence of Lord Malmesbury, who had been one of his guardians. His duties as such were, as he tells us, confined to the signing of his name. The Duke of Portland was the Prime Minister, but Mr. Canning was Secretary of State for Foreign Affairs and gave the Ministry what power it had. Soon afterwards, still in 1807, application was made to Canning to appoint young Palmerston Under-Secretary of State for Foreign Affairs, but the place had already been given away. A quarter of a century was thus left to run by, as Mr. Ashley remarks, before he took his place in that department.

It was Under the Duke of Portland, as a special friend and follower of Canning, that Lord Palmerston took his place as a Government servant, in April, 1807. As such he remained, with six intervals, amounting in all to about nine years, till on 16th October, 1865, he died at Brocket Hall, in Hertfordshire, in the same house in which Lord Melbourne, whose brother-in-law he became, had previously died in 1848. For four or five months of his life,—in the winter of 1834-35,—he was without a seat in Parliament, till in the April of that year he found himself landed in a safe refuge in Tiverton. At the time at which he entered the Admiralty he was not yet twenty-three years old. He possessed a fair patrimony, but was by no means a rich nobleman. He had an Irish property in County Sligo, partly in the town, but chiefly on the sea-coast. To this he paid great attention. I remember having been told on the spot nearly forty years ago that that wonderful "Irishman," Lord Palmerston, had for the last ten years spent all his income upon the estate. He had just then been over, and the beauty of his presence had probably enhanced the virtue of his operations. The family house was at Broadlands, near Romsey, in Hampshire. Here he went into the country, sometimes for a week or two at a time, whereas other country gentlemen go for months. Nothing astonishes us more than the smallness of the periods allowed to himself by Lord Palmerston for the amusements of life. But he makes his statements in that respect without any feeling either of surprise or self-praise. He does in one place break out into anger against a keeper who spends his nights in the alehouse in order that the poachers may spend theirs in the coverts. "Five guns killing sixteen pheasants in Yew Tree!" Yew Tree we presume to have been a wood, and certainly must have been unsatisfactory even in 1834, when the catastrophe took place. The Foreign Secretary going down to his own preserves with four friends, and for a very short holiday, and finding only three birds apiece among them, cannot but have been exasperating! But Mr. Thresher, the keeper in fault, probably thought that a man so greatly occupied with foreign affairs as his master, could not want many pheasants.

❑❑❑

CHAPTER II

Palmerston as Junior Lord of the Admiralty and Secretary of War, April, 1807, to May, 1827

THE early years of Lord Palmerston, though he was in office, in Parliament, even when he had become a Cabinet Minister, were not those by which he will be known. Pitt died about the age at which Palmerston went to the Foreign Office, having served his country as Prime Minister for nearly twenty years. But during that period of his comparative youth, Lord Palmerston was always at work, gaining slowly that consideration in the eyes of men on which his fame and strength was built up. It was not in him to take Parliament by surprise, and to captivate the ears of all hearers by some precocious speech. Nevertheless he slowly learned the art of speaking with great efficiency, and could at last carry on a debate with energy and success,—as was found by the Don Pacifico speech, to which we shall come in his sixty-sixth year, when he spoke for five consecutive hours. In the way of speech-making, that was the greatest effort of his life; but other orators have reached their zenith before they have become sexagenarians. Through his whole life I think that he had never spoken for the mere sake of the effect which oratory is supposed to have. In the mode of life to which he had fashioned himself, there constantly arose matters which required speeches. When the occasion fell upon him he could express himself. When, as Secretary of War, he had to advocate a Military College, he declared that, "for his part, he wished to see the British soldier with a British character, with British habits, with a British education, and with as little as possible of anything foreign." The argument was *ad captandum*, but it was of a nature fitted for its purpose. Such generally were his arguments. And he could tell a story with expressive force, as he did tell the story of Don Pacifico in his own defence. He failed lamentably in defending himself after his dismissal from the Foreign Office,—when the witty statesman said, prematurely, that there "had been a Palmerston." Defence by words would at that moment have been very difficult,—to have been efficacious and hot to have been disloyal! But he could answer a rowdy at the hustings with rough, easy fun, in a manner that, with such an audience, was found to be successful. He seems to have prepared his speeches carefully when he was young, having among his papers left the notes behind him when he died, but to have abandoned the practice as he became accustomed to the work. It was just what we should have expected. He looked forward as a young man to speaking as a necessity from which there could be no escape; but he never seems to have regarded the art as the source of his power, or the bulwark of his fame.

His first speech was in 1808, on the taking of Copenhagen. We have all read our history sufficiently to know that Nelson raised his telescope to his blind eye, or in other words, took upon himself to disobey his superior officer. The Danish expedition was debated, and Nelson, as we know, got great honour for what would have ruined him had he been unsuccessful. The Ministry were attacked as to the expedition to Copenhagen, and on this occasion Lord Palmerston, as a Lord of the Admiralty, made his first speech. "My dear Elizabeth," he says, writing to his sister, "you will see by this day's paper that I was tempted by some evil spirit to make a fool of myself for the entertainment of the House last night; however I thought it was a good opportunity of breaking the ice, although one should flounder a little in doing so; as it was impossible to talk any egregious nonsense in so good a cause." In time, as he came to have more experience, he must have found that in this he was in error. Let the case be ever so good, the oratory may be bad. But he had numbers on his side. There were 253 votes for Government and 108 against it;—and yet Palmerston complained to his sister that the division was not so good as he had expected. He tells us he was half an hour on his legs, and did "not feel so much alarmed as I expected to be."

He had opened his lips but once in the House of Commons, when, in October 1809, there came a break up of the Cabinet, on the duel between Canning and Castlereagh. Mr. Percival undertook the office of Prime Minister, and offered to Palmerston the place of Chancellor of the Exchequer, from the duties of which he was desirous of saving himself. The fact that he did so will chiefly be of use to us as showing the idea which was then held of Lord Palmerston by his elders, and the idea which he held himself. He writes to Lord Malmesbury for advice, but he himself gives the advice on which he means to act "I have always thought it unfortunate for any one, and particularly a young man, to be put above his proper level, as he only rises to fall the lower. Now, I am quite without knowledge of finance, and never but once spoke in the House." "A good deal of debating must of course devolve upon the person holding the Chancellorship of the Exchequer. All persons, not born with the talents of Pitt or Fox, must make many bad speeches at first, if they speak a great deal on many subjects, as they cannot be masters of all; and a bad speech, though tolerated in any person not in a responsible situation, would make a Chancellor of the Exchequer exceedingly ridiculous." And so that matter of the Chancellorship of the Exchequer was decided. He had not possessed the gifts which would have enabled him to be a second Pitt, but he had the gift of knowing that he could not be so. He settled down at last as Secretary at War, and, by his own judgment, decided on taking the office without a seat in the Cabinet. Writing again to Lord Malmesbury, he says: "Percival having very handsomely given me the option of the Cabinet with the War Office (if I go to it), I thought it best on the whole to decline it; and I trust that, although you seemed to be of a different opinion at first, you will not, on the whole, think I was wrong." He tells us that he entered on his new functions on the 27th of October, 1809. He was then twenty-five years old.

Having thus made his choice against the Cabinet, he did not enter those sacred doors till May, 1827. An apprenticeship of eighteen years was more, probably, than he had anticipated when he made his choice. But it was no doubt well for his future fame and his stability as a Government servant, that it should have been so. During these eighteen years he was thoroughly learning his duty as a Minister of the Crown;—learning, as some will say, how to exaggerate those duties, and to absorb into his own hands more of power and potentiality than had been intended by those who had appointed him. But by himself, though he thought probably but little about it while he was learning it, the lesson had to be learned; and the lesson taught seems to have been this, that he would interfere with the duties of no other office than his own, but with those duties he would put up with no interference. There may have been danger in this; but such was his theory of official life. And it can hardly be denied that as a Minister of State no Englishman has been more successful.

Than Mr. Percival, who thus offered to Lord Palmerston a seat in his Cabinet, no Englishman who has become Prime Minister, was ever a more prejudiced, more antiquated Tory. He was, especially, a determined Protestant, regarding any Catholic claims to the privileges of citizenship with all the bigotry of religious conviction. At this time the Regency began, King George III. having given place to his son, who became Prince Regent, and ten years afterwards George IV. But in Lord Palmerston's early speeches, or in his parliamentary conduct, there is no allusion to any peculiar political bias, and apparently no thought of it. He had joined the Government, as other young men in lower ranks of life join this or the other profession, and as other young men do,—or neglect to do,—did the work that came to his hands. In none of his letters that are published does there appear any strong political feeling, as there would be nowadays, in the letters of young men who look to parliament for distinction. He had been brought up among Tories, and was therefore a Tory; but with no violence of predilection. He was keen rather as to the delights of the life of fashion in which he lived; but he seems to have known that such delights cease to be delightful if they be not accompanied by work, and therefore he worked, having always before his eyes the future which might possibly be open to him,—and which did eventually come to him. Throughout the next twenty years he will be found constant at his office, for the most part silent in Parliament, but speaking, when he did speak, always with a mind gradually, but very gently, tending towards liberal principles.

Then there came a change in the Government. In May, 1812, Mr. Percival was murdered in the lobby of the House of Commons, and Lord Liverpool became Prime Minister. Under him there came a period of so great a glory for England that the weakness of his administration has been forgotten in the military annals of the country. But Lord Palmerston held his place as Secretary at War till 1827, and, on the death of Lord Liverpool, he came into the Cabinet. That such a man as Lord Liverpool should have been head of the Government for fifteen years is not more wonderful than that such another as Lord Palmerston should during the same long period have filled a subordinate office under him. And during this time Waterloo had taken place, and the occupation of Paris. But our concern is here with the subordinate, and not with the Prime Minister. He had at last been elected by the University of Cambridge in 1812, and was re-elected in 1818, 1820, and 1825. Very little is heard of him during the whole of this period as a public man, and yet it was by his mouth that the taxes were suggested by which the enormous war estimates and foreign subsidies of 1813, 1814, and 1815 were supplied. He seems to have submitted tamely to whatever Lord Liverpool proposed, and to have considered that, if he did his duty according to his own theory in his own office, he need not trouble his head with the political feelings of other members of the Government. He contested with Sir David Dundas and the Duke of York the question of the power and supremacy which was invested in them as Commanders-in-Chief, and in himself as Secretary of War, with a determination of purpose quite worthy of the future Foreign Secretary. On these occasions neither did the Commander-in-Chief nor the Secretary at War gain any victory, the Prime Minister of the day feeling himself to be too weak to decide against either disputant; but

Palmerston seems to have held his own and to have well maintained the prestige and influence of his office.

When the name of "Cupid" was first given to him I am unable to learn, but it was probably during this period, and tells a tale only of the sort of life which he then led. He was the "enfant gâté" of society; but he was not "spoiled" as regarded his official and parliamentary duties. He was called "Cupid," and enjoyed a peculiar popularity in all assemblies in which fashion held the sway. Men seemed to believe in him, and women too, as having a position peculiarly his own.

He was a member of a Tory Government, and yet since 1812 had voted in favour of the Catholics whenever questions in their favour came before the House. It seems that in 1825, when at a general election he had to stand again for the University, he expected that the influence of the Government would be given to Copley,—the future Lord Lyndhurst,—and to Goulburn. "I had complained," he said, "to Lord Liverpool and the Duke of Wellington and Canning, of being attacked, in violation of the understanding upon which the Government was formed, and by which the Catholic question was to be an open one; and I told Lord Liverpool that if I was beaten I should quit the Government. This was the first decided step towards a breach between me and the Tories, and they were the aggressors." And that the influence of the Government was so given there can be no doubt, as Copley came in at the head of the poll; but still, as Lord Palmerston was enabled to keep his seat, he and Lord Liverpool went on together in office as long as Lord Liverpool remained. "The Whigs have behaved most handsomely to me," he says further on; "they have given me hearty and cordial support, and, in fact, bring me in. Liverpool has acted as he always does to a friend on personal questions,—shabbily, timidly and ill. If I am beat, I have told him he must find another Secretary at War, for I certainly will not continue in office."

During this long period we have glimpses of his life from letters to his sister Elizabeth and to his brother William, who was afterwards for some years our Minister at Naples. He went to Paris soon after Waterloo, but not till the Sovereigns and the Duke of Wellington had decided on surrendering to their old owners those works of art which Napoleon had brought to Paris. "But I rejoice most exceedingly in the thing, and would have foregone the sight of every work of art in the gallery sooner than have left them there. The French, however,—that is, the Royalists,—are furious; and Lady Malmesbury, who lives almost entirely with them, has taken it up in so tragical a tone that literally there is no talking of it to her. She says the Duke has disgraced himself, that it is *impossible* for him to stay in Paris, and that it *must* end in the murder of all the English. When first she talked to me about it, I felt like a person who is holding his countenance for a wager while somebody tickles his nose; and when, in spite of all my endeavours, a smirking smile crept into my face, she said, in the most serious manner, 'No, indeed, this is no laughing matter; I can assure you it is very serious indeed! The Netherland pictures are gone. The Austrians are beginning to take the Italian school belonging to them; and then the Pope takes his property. The statues will go after the pictures, and the horses are to be taken down to-day or to-morrow!'"

In 1818 Palmerston was shot at as he was entering his office, by a madman, one Lieutenant Davis; and I remember well to have had the spot pointed out some ten years afterwards, and to have heard the story that it was chiefly by his own quickness of movement that his life was saved. We have been told since that he supplied the money necessary for the defence of the culprit. He afterwards visited Waterloo, and criticizes the dirt of the Russian troops whom he saw reviewed there. He finds fault also with the reasons given for the building of a fortress at Namur, thinking that this displayed an absence of proper military spirit "I am afraid," he says, "that our allies the Belgians want much of that spirit never to submit or yield, which is necessary to enable them successfully to defend their territory." Here we do not quite agree with his criticism, and can only express our hope, as we pass on, that the Belgians may continue to do their work as well for the next fifty years as they have done for the last. Then we come across a remark as to an old friend of ours, which the light of subsequent years has proved to be altogether wrong. Speaking of the army estimates, he says:

"He"—Joseph Hume—"is going down hill very fast; indeed, so dull and blunder-headed a fellow, notwithstanding all his perseverance and application, could not long hold his own in the House of Commons." Joseph Hume, however, did hold his ground, and rose till he was believed in as the great financial reformer of the House of Commons.

The style of Palmerston's letters is what one would expect from that of his speeches and despatches. It is clear, concise, and very easy to understand, without any approach to artificial graces, or even to the formalities of grammatical correctness. "As to weather, we are fried alive." He mixes up his racing and his property, his art and his politics, just as any other man would do. "I have been a horrid bad correspondent for some time past." But he goes at length into his land improvements, and tells his reader, with great zeal, of the good he has been doing down in Co. Sligo: "My harbour is nearly completed;—it will be an excellent one for my purposes; it will be about one and a quarter English acres in extent, and will have fourteen feet water at high spring tides,—enough depth to admit vessels of 300 tons, and as much as any harbour on the west coast of Ireland; and it has an excellent anchorage in front of it, where ships may wait the tide to enter. I have no doubt that in a short time it will be much frequented by the coasting trade; and if I can get people—which Nimmo thinks probable—to lay down a railway to it from the end of Loch Erne, a distance of fourteen English miles, it would become the exporting and importing harbour for a large tract of very fertile country lying on the banks of that lake, and would communicate with an inland navigation of nearly forty miles in extent." The Nimmo named is the engineer of those days who did much good work in the West of Ireland. "I have established an infant linen market at Cliffony, held once a month, and have no doubt of its prospering and increasing. I have just got two schools on foot, but am at war with my priest, who, as usual, forbids the people to send their children."

The battle for Catholic Emancipation was being carried on, and it became clearer from year to year on which side Lord Palmerston was to be counted, in spite of his colleagues, whom he thus names: "I can forgive old women like the Chancellor, spoonies like Liverpool, ignoramuses like Westmoreland, old stumped-up Tories like Bathurst; but how such a man as Peel, liberal, enlightened, and fresh-minded, should find himself running in such a pack is hardly intelligible. I think he must in his heart regret those early pledges and youthful prejudices which have committed him to opinions so different from the comprehensive and statesmanlike views which he takes of foreign affairs." But even for Catholic Emancipation he had very little to say in Parliament. It cannot be too often declared,—either as against his character as a statesman or on his behalf, as the reader may think it,—that he was not in any part of his career a man prone to speech. He was brought up in that school of politicians in which a man uses his power of speech, or used to use it, not as a woman uses her teeth, for ornament, but as a dog does, for attack and defence. To have to make a speech was from the first to the last of his career an evil thing, though the evil became mitigated by practice, till as a personal annoyance it wore away. Nevertheless there was the time lost, and the trouble necessary to be taken, and the hours given up to the listening to other people, which might have been so satisfactorily employed either in reading or writing, or in early years in playing Cupid, or even in shooting pheasants, if his keeper would preserve them for him! As for his taking delight in the speeches of others, it cannot be believed of him. Once—but he was then very young—did he burst out into praise of Canning's eloquence. "Canning's speech was one of the most brilliant I ever heard. He carried the House with him throughout." But at that time he was not yet twenty-four.

When Lord Liverpool died he was forty. And he had lived as a man conspicuous in the world,—in office the whole time, holding a rank there next to that of the Cabinet, remarkable for his official carefulness, for his industry, for his resolution to let nothing pass without his notice. Soon after he had joined the War Office, in 1809, he had remarked on the insufficiency of the departmental resources. "Its inadequacy to get through the current business that comes before it is really a disgrace to the country; and the arrear of regimental accounts unsettled is of a magnitude not to be conceived. We are now working at the Treasury, to induce them to agree to a plan, proposed originally by Sir James Pulteney and reconsidered by Granville Leveson, by which, I think, we shall provide for the current business, and the arrear must then be got rid of as well as we can contrive to do it." But he had clung to his work during the whole period with that tenacity which in official life will get the better of all arrears. And in doing so he had made his character known to all official men. It was not because he was a good speaker, as is now generally the case, that he was chosen by one Minister after another, and that Lord Liverpool had been so anxious to retain him, but because the office work was safe in his hands, and because he had shown that he would make fewer mistakes than another man. He had always the pluck to stand up for himself and his office in a becoming manner, caring nothing for any, whether they were in opposition, or below him in office or above; whether they were in the Cabinet or of royal blood, as was the Duke of York. "Come on then and fight, if it has to be." This is what he would say, with all good-humour; but had never any special desire to have his official points and aspirations and beliefs made matter of debate in either House of Parliament. Such was his official character, and joined to this was his fame as a man of fashion. He did all things that young men did, and did them well, and at forty he was still a young man. Or if he did not do them well, he did them as a young man of fashion ought to do them. If he was not at first successful with his racing, he carried on the amusement in the grand manner. He did not bet. It was not the fashion for a nobleman in those days to plunge. But he kept his horses with a first-class trainer, and was careful to see that the stable as far as possible was made to pay its expenses. We can imagine that he was much thought of at Almack's, and was a desired guest at the houses of all the exquisites. There is little, or indeed nothing, said about his tailors or bootmakers in any of his letters that have come to us. But we can imagine that he was very careful in his dress, without descending to the outspoken vanity of dandyism. He lived a life full to overflowing in every direction, and on which the society of beautiful women must have had great effect.

But with beautiful women he got into no troubles. There exists at least no record of such trouble. He passed on, a young man of fashion, for a period of twenty years, sipping all the honey from all the flowers, but without any of the usual consequences of such sipping. It was characteristic of him that neither in his early or in his later life was there any love of display. He was a man desirous of all things that were pleasant, but seems to have wished that they should be accorded to him simply as his deserts, and not in obedience to any demand that he had made for them. In 1827, when he was nearly forty-three years old, he was called into the Cabinet. This formed the dividing point in his life, up to which I have regarded him as a young man, and after which I will not call him by that name though it may have been deserved. But I will ask my readers to remark that when that time came he had already a long time since refused to be a Cabinet Minister; refused to be Chancellor of the Exchequer; had twice refused to be Governor-General of India; had refused to be the Governor of Jamaica, an office for which George IV. seems to have thought him peculiarly qualified; and refused to be Postmaster-General, a place which in those days required the holder to be a peer. But of the records of his life up to that period little is but now thought, and even yet three years more had to run by, and the discreet age of forty-six had to be reached, before he was placed at the Foreign Office, in the administration of which department he will, I think, be best known in history.

❑❑❑

CHAPTER III

Secretary at War, With Seat in the Cabinet

IT is a great thing to be a Cabinet Minister. Every man when he begins a life of politics feels that. He feels it when he gets into Parliament, and when he joins a Government in some subordinate office. It is the goal to which his hopes aspire, and the success to which his ambition ventures to look. The young politician hardly expects to be Prime Minister, but he does, within his own bosom, think it possible that he may achieve an entrance within those doors which enclose that mysterious entity which we call the Cabinet. The Cabinet is essentially English in its abnormal constitution, having grown to its present enormous responsibility without any written rules or defined powers. There is nothing to prescribe its numbers, which do indeed vary very greatly; nor indeed is there any law requiring that this or that officer of the Government should be a member of it,—as there is no law by which its very existence is made necessary. It is considered essential that the Chancellor and the Secretaries of State should be of the Cabinet, but we have no law which would be broken were it to be completed without them. But it is understood by all men that the governing of the country is in the hands of a small junta of individuals who form the Cabinet, and it is equally well understood that all members of the Government who are not in the Cabinet are responsible for nothing beyond the proper performances of their own official duties; though they, too, are bound to resign when their betters resign, and are bound also to support their betters by parliamentary aid and judicious backing in all but the very few matters which are regarded as "open questions." In fact, the Cabinet Minister is a governing power, and the Minister not in the Cabinet is simply the servant of the Premier. It is therefore undoubtedly the ambition of every political servant of his country to make good his claim to a seat in the Cabinet. And although there may now be some little advance in the thorough distinction of the two places since the days in which Lord Palmerston was first enlisted as a servant of the Crown, rather more than seventy years ago, yet even then the feeling as to the power of the Cabinet Minister existed as it does now. It has been told how, in 1809, Mr. Percival offered to make Lord Palmerston Chancellor of the Exchequer. "Annexed to this office he offered a seat in the Cabinet, if I chose it," he said in a letter to Lord Malmesbury, asking for advice. "And he thought it better I should have it. I, of course, expressed to him how much honoured I felt by this very flattering proof of the good opinion he was pleased to entertain of me; but also my great fears that I should find myself wholly incompetent for the situation, both from my inexperience in the details of matters of finance, and my want of practice in public speaking." From this we see how much surprised Lord Palmerston had himself been by the offer. But with that wonderful reliance on his own power which always marked him, and which was as conspicuous when he doubted his power as when he relied on it, he declined the offer. And he added, "A bad speech, though tolerated in any person not in a responsible situation, would make a Chancellor of the Exchequer exceedingly ridiculous, particularly if his friends could not set off against his bad oratory a great knowledge and capacity for business." Actuated by these reasons, Lord Palmerston declined the offer, and then came into office simply as Secretary at War without a seat in the Cabinet. His self-diffidence was repaid by sixteen years of comparative exclusion. Mr. Percival had been murdered, and Lord Liverpool, who became Prime Minister in Mr. Percival's place, had either thought less of Lord Palmerston or had been thought less of by him. The fact probably was that as Palmerston grew in years he had learned to discard many of the ideas of Toryism, and that he became year by year less palatable to so thorough a Tory as was Lord Liverpool. Be that as it may, we can fancy that before he reached the age of forty-three he must occasionally have looked back with watering lips at that offer which had once been made to him. Governor-Generalships and peerages were not to his taste. Such rich rewards would have removed him from that central and busy life which he intended for himself in the House of Commons. But the fruition of the central and busy life, though it had been offered to him young, had been long delayed before it came again within his grasp. I can fancy that he must have felt this, though in his letters there is no word of baulked expectations or of disappointed hopes. He took it all as it came, resolving to be useful after his kind, and resolving also to be powerful. Wherever he might be, he would be interfered with by none, by Kings or Kaisers, by Prime Ministers or Commanders-in-Chief, nor would he interfere with any others in their line. I am far from saying that in this manner a servant of his country, who is anxious to be useful rather than powerful, may best do his duty. Lord Palmerston was a man with whom it must often have been difficult for a colleague to serve. The lines of demarcation between one officer and another, and between one class of duty and another class, are not so plain as to make it easy if practicable, or to make it always pleasant; but this was a man with whom such a theory was a determined principle, and acting upon that he went to the end with greater success than might have been possible in the hands of another. He had shown his stubbornness even when not in the Cabinet, and now that he was to be in the Cabinet, it was not probable that he would become more malleable than before. I do not say that a determination so to act had come from that process of mind which we call thinking a thing out. It was not in his nature to think many things out beyond the matters which he had in hand; but given the matter, it was so that he acted. In a book just published,[F] the author speaks of "the childish perversity which marked Lord Palmerston's dealings with Greece in these years, from his stubborn defence of Count Armansperg down to his disputes about etiquette." This perversity was an essential part of Lord Palmerston's character,—and of his strength.

In 1827 Lord Liverpool died, and new arrangements of the Cabinet and Government became necessary. Mr. Canning was selected as Prime Minister, and proceeded to form that combination which led to the adoption of Catholic Emancipation in 1829, and to the passing of the Reform Bill in 1832. It has been customary to say that certain of the Whig party joined the Tories when Mr. Canning became Prime Minister. But it would perhaps be more correct to describe that which then took place as a fusion in the minds of men caused by natural changes, as in the course of years the old Tory convictions gave way to new ideas as to the liberty of the subject. The last really Tory Government in England, which had now become extinct, was that of Lord Liverpool and Lord Eldon; and even their Toryism grows pale when compared with that of the Ministers who had assisted George III. in taxing the Americans.

When Mr. Canning became Prime Minister, he was desirous of keeping the seals of the Foreign Office in his own hands, and with this object offered to Lord Palmerston the place of Chancellor of the Exchequer, with a seat in the Cabinet. This Lord Palmerston at first accepted. But there were difficulties in the way. "George IV., who personally hated me," said Lord Palmerston, "did not fancy me as Chancellor of the Exchequer. He wanted to have Herries in that office." Whether this be true or not, or whether Canning changed his mind, the arrangement was never carried out. "Some weeks after this Canning sent for me again, to say he had a proposition to make to me, which he should not himself have thought of, but that the King had said he knew, and was sure, that it was just the very thing I should like, and that was to go as Governor to Jamaica. I laughed so heartily that I observed Canning looked quite put out, and I was obliged to grow serious again." Canning then offered him the Governor-Generalship of India; but Lord Palmerston refused, with sundry excuses as to his health (which he would by no means allow when the same office was offered by him many years afterwards to Canning's son), and alleging, also, that he had no family for whom he was desirous of amassing a fortune. In the end a Cabinet was made up by expedients intended only to be temporary. Canning was Chancellor of the Exchequer as well as First Lord of the Treasury; Lord Granville, retaining his embassy at Paris, became for the time Secretary of State for Foreign Affairs; Palmerston, still keeping some hold on the Chancellorship of the Exchequer for the future, remained Secretary at War, but with the additional plum that he was to have the patronage of the army, no new Commander-in-Chief having been appointed in place of the Duke of Wellington, who had thought it necessary to resign with his brother Tories. "As to the Tories, who would hardly vote for our measures before, we must not look for any cordial support from them now. Not but that, by degrees and one by one, they will all by instinct come round to the oat-sieve." Come round to the oat-sieve! Alas, it is sad to see a public servant, who had already served his country for nearly twenty years, and who was yet destined to serve it for forty years more, speaking in such language of those by whom Cabinets are formed! But though we may believe it of Lord Eldon, we do not believe it of the Duke of Wellington or of Sir Robert Peel,—three of the men of whom Lord Palmerston was then speaking; nor, in truth, do we believe it of Lord Palmerston himself.

Of this period of Lord Palmerston's life, we have the record left to us in a partial autobiography which he drew out afterwards, and which has been made known to us by Lord Dalling. In reference to this autobiography, the memory of Lord Palmerston has been laden with some reproach, which seems not altogether to be undeserved when we look at the purposes for which it has been used. But we must remember that it was not written, like the journal by which it is preceded, at the time of the occurrences which it relates, but many years afterwards, when it was prepared, probably at the request of Lord Dalling to whom it was at any rate given by Lady Palmerston. Mr. Herries had been Chancellor of the Exchequer in Lord Goderich's Administration. In this autobiography the name of Mr. Herries is mentioned with disrespect,—and we must certainly say with inaccuracy, after the defence which has lately been published by his sons. This vindication has been occasioned, as is stated in the first words of the memoir,[G] by the appearance of Mr. Spencer Walpole's "History of England," and is an attack on Mr. Walpole rather than on Lord Palmerston. But Mr. Walpole has founded his objectionable assertion partly on Lord Palmerston's words; and though we may think ourselves entitled to declare that Lord Dalling should be made accountable for inaccuracies so published, and not the writer of an autobiography, who after nearly forty years has trusted to his memory when his journal failed him, still there are the written words, not intentionally false when written, but still imbued with that venom to which political feelings are at any rate as subject now as they were then.

The passage in the autobiography of which complaint is made was as follows. The period alluded to is the formation of the Cabinet by Canning on Lord Liverpool's death, the spring, namely, of 1827. "In the meanwhile intrigues were set on foot. George IV., who personally hated me, did not fancy me as Chancellor of the Exchequer. He wanted to have Herries in that office. There were questions about palaces and crown lands which the King was very anxious about, and he wished either to have a creature of his own in the Exchequer, or to have the office of Chancellor of the Exchequer held by the First Lord, whose numerous occupations would compel him to leave details very much to George Harrison, the Secretary, and to Herries, Auditor of the Civil List." To this a note is appended by Lord Dalling, stating that Mr. Herries was also Joint Secretary of the Treasury. One sees here the acrimony displayed by the Whig of the day in which it was written against the Tory King and the Tory financier, whose party he had already left. But the character of George IV. suffers more than that of Mr. Herries from the words of the autobiographer. An insinuation about the "palaces and crown lands" is no doubt made, which we surrender to the filial feelings of Sir Charles and Mr. Herries. To have heard such words quoted from the old memoirs of an old man is fairly admitted by them both not to have required such a measure of vindication as a book,—which is, however, quite able to justify itself by its own merits. It is their use, when taken from Lord Dalling's book, and applied to purposes of history, that has caused their indignation.

But it was after this, in August and September, 1827, after Mr. Canning's death, and when Lord Goderich was the Prime Minister elect, that the contest with the King went on as to the appointment of Mr. Herries. Here, in lieu of the autobiography, we have Lord Palmerston's letters, as to the actual truth of which no doubt is raised. There existed evidently one of those insoluble knots, which have to be cut at last by him who has the greatest power. The King did want Herries to be Chancellor of the Exchequer, and was anxious to have as many Tories as might be possible in the mixed Government for which he had given his authority. "The King wants Herries to be Chancellor of the Exchequer. The Whigs object to him pointedly, and Goderich wishes to have me. Neither party will give way." That is quoted from a letter from Lord Palmerston to his brother, and it is at any rate true. It ended in the weakest man giving way, for Lord Goderich was told "to go home and take care of himself." The Duke became Prime Minister, with Goulburn for his Chancellor of the Exchequer, and Mr. Herries became Master of the Mint.

Canning died on the 8th of August, and all these arrangements were more short-lived than had been intended. Lord Goderich, as stated above, became Prime Minister, but retained his place only a few months—with no effect on Lord Palmerston's immediate work, except that he ceased to hold the patronage of the army, the Duke of Wellington becoming again Commander-in-Chief. In our days it is presumed that the head of the army shall exercise no political power, and in no wise be guided by political exigencies. But that was not the Duke's understanding. He had declined to serve under Mr. Canning, thus leaving the office for a while vacant. But now that Canning was gone he was reappointed. "He comes in without any stipulations or conditions whatever," Lord Palmerston said to his brother; and in his autobiography he tells a story of the Duke and Lord Anglesey. Lord Anglesey, on behalf of the Government, had been sent to invite the Duke to resume the office. "Well, gentlemen, I have done what you sent me to do," he said on his return. "I have brought you the Duke of Wellington's acceptance as Commander-in-Chief, and, by God, mark my words; as sure as you are alive he will trip up all your party before six months are over your heads." "But it was the King who did it," continued Lord Palmerston.

Early in 1828 the Duke succeeded Lord Goderich as Prime Minister; but though going in as a Tory, he took with him the leading members of Mr. Canning's party, who may be regarded as the Liberals of those days,—as men who had at any rate learned to lean towards Liberalism in the course of the training they had received. These were Lord Dudley and Ward, Mr. Huskisson, Mr. Grant, and Lord Palmerston. But more to be noted than any such members of the Duke's Government was the fact that Lord Eldon was not a member. Lord Lyndhurst was the Lord Chancellor instead of Lord Eldon. Lord Lyndhurst had been Lord Chancellor under Lord Goderich and Mr. Canning; but that was to have been expected. Mr. Canning had not intended to defend his country from Roman Catholic aggression; but the Duke would surely do so; and under the Duke's leading Mr. Peel, who, as Home Secretary, would lead the House of Commons, would surely assist in such work. And were there not Lord Bathurst and Lord Ellenborough and Mr. Goulburn in the Cabinet? Though Palmerston and Huskisson were to be there, Lord Eldon's hopes ran high. But the time for Lord Eldon had passed by. He was probably the last of the English Statesmen who could not under any circumstances have been got to vote for the smallest amount of political relief to a Roman Catholic. In all descriptions of politicians of those days, we see men defined as being Catholic or the reverse, and men also sometimes are called "Protestants." Lord Eldon was especially a "Protestant;" as Lord Palmerston, and soon afterwards the Duke of Wellington and Peel were "Catholics." The great political question of the present day was the expediency of lessening in some degree "Catholic" disabilities. And when Cabinets were formed, men were admitted or the reverse according to their "Catholic" proclivities. Lord Palmerston during his official career had gradually become "Catholic"; and it was well known of him now that, let him enter what Government he might, he would do so pledged to support the Catholics.

Lord Palmerston was now to go out of office and to remain for two years in opposition; but the circumstances of his going were of a nature to bring about a violent decision of the "Catholic" claims, though it cannot be said that he himself was in any way responsible for doing so. There came up some dispute in the Cabinet as to the disfranchisement of East Retford and Penryn, in the course of which Mr. Huskisson resigned. Mr. Huskisson was the follower of Mr. Canning. That the Duke and Mr. Huskisson should not have been easy together in the same Cabinet we can understand; but we are told that Mr. Huskisson was anxious that his resignation should not be accepted. The Duke, however, was determined that he should go, and would hear nothing of any mistake made as to the letter of resignation. "It was not a mistake," he said; "it is not a mistake; and it shall not be a mistake." The consequence was that with Mr. Huskisson three other members resigned, Lord Dudley and Ward, Lord Palmerston, and Mr. Grant. Now Mr. Grant, who was President of the Board of Trade, was followed in that office by Mr. Vesey Fitzgerald, the member for County Clare. The County Clare thus became vacant, and, declining to re-elect Mr. Fitzgerald, returned Mr. O'Connell in his place; and thus the Roman Catholic question was forced upon the country. The three or four gentlemen who filled the vacant places in the Duke of Wellington's Cabinet were of course Tories; and in this way a Tory Government, *pur et simple*, was again established. But it was not such a Tory Government as that presided over by Lord Liverpool, and in which Lord Eldon kept the conscience of the King.

At this time Lord Palmerston had already taken much interest in foreign affairs, and we find him explaining in his letters to his brother how stood the Portuguese affairs, and Spanish, and Austrian, and Greek, and Turkish. It is not necessary, in this short memoir, to explain how the Turkish and Egyptian fleets had been destroyed at Navarino by us and our allies, seeing that Lord Palmerston had not been concerned in the matter. But it is pleasant to see, in looking over the details as given in his life, how anxious he already was for freedom in Portugal and in Greece, and how steadily he was opposed to Prince Metternich and Austrian obstinacy. Three or four articles of that creed, to which he was true during his whole life, now crop up. These, we should say, were Catholic emancipation and the maintenance of English influence at home and abroad, and, above all things, the suppression of the slave trade. Greece was then fighting for the possession of herself, and Lord Palmerston was eager that we should take her part. He was as strongly opposed to Turkey in oppressing Greece as he was eager afterwards in defending Turkey from Russian oppression. But in all these matters he spoke and wrote with an evident desire that England should be supreme; and, though he was no more concerned in them than as one of an entire Cabinet which was concerned, he was forming that character in which we find it difficult to say whether he was hereafter most to be blamed as a bully or to be praised as a patriot. Had he brought England into disgrace or suffering, or, worse still, to ruin, the question would have answered itself. He would have gone down the valley of time nearly forgotten, and this little book would never have been written. But he played his game boldly, and dared to run the risk of dismissal, of personal hatred, and perhaps of impeachment. From first to last he played it successfully, and has obtained the goodwill of his countrymen, high reputation throughout Europe, and a fame which is due rather to his courage than his genius.

Now, in 1828, Lord Palmerston was out of office for the first time since he had become a Lord of the Admiralty in 1807. There had been twenty-one years of it, during which he had been thoroughly used to official life, official habits, and official language. It must have seemed to him that a man such as he was born to be in office. "It is so many years since I have been entirely my own master," he writes, "that I feel it quite comical to have no tie, and to be able to dispose of my day as I like." Then he goes on to tell how, since he had left the Duke of Wellington's Government, the Duke of Clarence had been specially civil to him, and the Duke of Cumberland specially uncivil; the two Royal brothers thus showing the politics by which they were instigated. We also know that the Duke of Clarence, afterwards William IV., sided with the Whigs, and that the Duke of Cumberland was the most violent of Tories. Lord Palmerston had hitherto been a Tory, but each of the Royal Dukes saw in what course he was about to run. "His next appearance in office," says Mr. Ashley, "was in connexion with the Whigs, and the whole of his subsequent career was spent in sympathy and harmony with their views."

It may be doubted whether this correctly describes the condition of Lord Palmerston's feelings. He was certainly loyal to the Whigs till his great fight came with Lord John Russell in 1851, when Lord John quarrelled with him, and not he with Lord John. And a thorough loyalty to a party of nearly a quarter of a century's duration may serve to make a man a Whig or Tory, as far as the name goes. Lord Palmerston had, almost by accident, fallen among the Whigs, having submitted himself to the genius of Mr. Canning, who, though influenced by liberal ideas, was no Whig; and then, on Canning's death, had leagued himself with Huskisson, upon whose shoulders as much of Canning's mantle had fallen as they were able to carry. Then Palmerston had left the Duke's Government because Huskisson left it, and had drifted away in a boat in which Charles Grant and William Lamb were with him. Thus he had joined himself with politicians who became Whig leaders and entertained Whig principles. But in doing so he was made over to the Foreign Office, where it was necessary that his politics should be foreign politics; and during those years of his life in which a man is most strongly imbued with political opinions,—from forty, let us say, till sixty, though in Lord Palmerston's case the twenty years came somewhat later,—his feelings and his opinions were British and conservative rather than liberal and expansive. He did not feel himself called upon to dispute the measures of his colleagues, but, in accordance with the system and theory by which he governed his own conduct, he confined himself to his own duties, and cared as little, we should say, for the Whiggery of Lord John Russell as for the Toryism of the Duke of Wellington and Lord Lyndhurst.

But, whether Whig or Tory, he was constant in doing good in that direction in which good done to himself must be good also to others. In the *Quarterly Review* for July, 1828, we are told what he did on his Irish estate in the way of draining;—"In the summer of 1826, a trial of what might be effected in reclaiming bog was made upon Lord Palmerston's estate. Fifty acres of bog, which contained nothing beneficial in the way of manure, were drained, and brought into a state fit for producing a crop, at an expense not exceeding £7 per acre; and in four months after the spade was put into it, says Mr. Nimmo, we had very fine potatoes, and turnips, and rape, and so on, growing there as good as on any land in the world." "We think the public in general, and the landed proprietors of Ireland in particular, are deeply indebted to Lord Palmerston for the experiment which he has made," says the reviewer. In these present days (1882) we can hardly venture to express a hope of the advantage which may accrue from such work to an Irish landlord; but such good when done is done for every one, whether to an owner of the soil or to another, and to Lord Palmerston the idea was rather that of multiplying the produce of the earth, than of an immediate increase to his own income.

We find from the autobiography how intent he was on the abolition of slavery in all parts of the earth, to which his own influence could be made to extend. The sale of Greek slaves by the Turks had been abominable. Men, women, and children had been abducted and sold. It was probably by the horrors which had been so occasioned, and which had been brought under his notice as Secretary at War, that this strong feeling was created; but it remained with him through his life; and, as Wilberforce and Buxton had been strong in speech to cause great things to be done, so was he constant in action to cause the perpetual doing of smaller things which in their aggregate became great. This, and the work of the Catholic emancipation,—which had begun in earnest with the Clare election,—occupied his mind during the time that he was out of office. But he went to Paris also during the same period, and wrote long letters home which, interesting as they are, would be too long for our present occasion.

In the autumn of 1830 we hear from himself what efforts were made to strengthen the Duke's Government,—efforts which ultimately led to the formation of Lord Grey's Ministry. The Duke of Wellington's

Government had been necessarily weak since the withdrawal from it of Mr. Canning's followers. Ministers had consented to the emancipation of the Catholics in 1829, and Mr. O'Connell had taken his seat for County Clare. Liberal ideas and Liberal measures were creeping on, and the Duke of Wellington felt that if he were desirous of keeping the Whigs out of office, and himself in, he could only do so by some re-admission of Mr. Canning's party. He accordingly sent an offer to Lord Palmerston. Would Lord Palmerston join him?

But that other, and greater, question of Reform of Parliament was now coming to the front. That the Duke of Wellington and Sir Robert Peel should not have already seen how impossible it was to stop the avalanche with such mill-dam as they were able to oppose to it is now surprising to us all. But we, looking back upon the avalanche, and what it did, can judge of its power much more accurately than could they who only heard its murmurings as it came. Wilson Croker, who was not the first messenger from the Duke, but who appeared afterwards on the scene, put to Lord Palmerston the one vital question;—"Are you resolved, or are you not, to vote for Parliamentary Reform?" "I am," said Lord Palmerston. "Then," said Croker, "there is no use in talking to you any more on this subject."

The Duke, finding it was so, resigned. There is nothing, I think, in Lord Palmerston's after-life to show that he himself loved the idea of Parliamentary Reform. But he had joined himself with Grant and Lamb, who had now become Lord Melbourne, and who, in truth, were now absolutely Whigs; and he had that power of foresight which enabled him to see which way the wind blew. He heard the rumblings of the avalanche, and determined not to be in its way when it should fall. Then Lord Grey's Government was formed, and Lord Palmerston became Foreign Secretary in November, 1830.

❑❑❑

CHAPTER IV

Palmerston Foreign Secretary, November, 1830, To November, 1834

WE here begin the record of that portion of Lord Palmerston's life which is of truth important to the English reader. In years, his life was more than half over. He was already forty-five, and had been in office for more than twenty years; but had he then died, he would have passed away as one of those unimportant statesmen whom, though they may do good work for their country, it is not worth their country's while to remember. But though he was forty-five, Lord Palmerston's period of importance was yet to begin, and to be continued during thirty-five additional years of uninterrupted labour.

Lord Dalling, in the short preface which he has prefixed to his unfinished life of Lord Palmerston, speaks as follows of the condition of England at this time in reference to the political state of Europe. "That period begins with a certain struggle against the resistance of the northern Cabinets to any change in the affairs of Europe; and a struggle at the same time against that reactionary spirit sprung from the Revolution of 1830 in France, which wished to change everything." The writer means to imply that England was anxious to stand between the despotism of Russia, Prussia, and Austria, and the democratic tendencies of France. In this he describes accurately the position which Lord Palmerston took as the exponent of English foreign politics, and which from the first to the last he maintained with a consistency which it has been given to few men to achieve, whose concern in the matter has lasted so long, and whose influence has been so great. Throughout his career it was his object to repress the personal power of the occupants of thrones; but at the same time so to repress that power as to give no inch of standing ground to demagogues. If that be true, it must be acknowledged that whether his attempts were good or evil, they were made in strict accordance with established English principles. And it will probably be admitted by most who may read these pages, that the efforts were good. That they were pre-eminently successful, it will be my duty to endeavour to show. That in making these efforts Lord Palmerston fell into various errors of manner, that he was frequently led away by human frailty, and often puffed up by pride and a spirit of personal success, is no doubt true. And it is true also that he seldom rose to any specially exalted view of human nature. He saw all things from a common-sense point of view, with what we may call mundane eyes. But we are not sure that such a point of view and such eyes are not the most useful for a British statesman. And of Lord Palmerston, it may be said that his followers would always know what political teaching they were expected to follow. He was not gifted with that fine insight into matters which enables a man to discern to-day something better than what he saw yesterday. Such still advancing improvement in sight is within the capacity only of the highest genius. But as an English politician can work only by the means of others, and needs many followers, the followers should see as quickly as he does, and if they be left in the dark they will not follow long. Lord Palmerston left none in the dark, and was therefore successful to the last by means of the true following of an attached party who always knew their man, and were sure that they never would be led whither they did not wish to go.

"As soon as Lord Grey was commissioned by the King to form an administration, he sent for me." These are the concluding words of that autobiography, of which mention has been made. Lord Grey sent for him, and he became Foreign Minister.

Writing to his brother on the 22nd of December, 1830, Lord Palmerston says; "I've been ever since my appointment like a man who has been plumped into a mill race, scarcely able by all his kicking and plunging to keep his head above water." We can understand that the kicking and plunging must have been very violent. The question had already arisen whether Belgium should or should not be made a kingdom of itself, with a king and constitution of its own. By the Treaty of Vienna in 1815 it had been decreed that for certain purposes which were in themselves no doubt wise, Belgium and Holland should be one. The United Provinces would be strong enough to form a barrier against the encroachments of France, and the balance of power in Europe and the maintenance of liberty might be so maintained. But the governing power had been left with the Dutch, and it was felt that the Dutch had oppressed the Belgians. The King of Holland had, as a temporary measure, assumed the power of appointing the judges in the two lands, and was unwilling to abandon it. He had then been assisted by the judges in depriving the Press of its liberty. And the Dutch had insisted that their language should be used in all public documents and all trials, although the Belgians had a language of their own, the Flemish language, and although French was the language of society, of the Courts and shops. And in all matters affecting religion and education, a strong bias was shown in favour of Protestant Holland over Catholic Belgium.

It can be understood that here in England feelings on this subject should run strong, and that the entire weight of the opposition to the new Government should be enlisted on the side of Protestant Holland. The Treaty of Vienna had been partly their work, and Lord Palmerston, who was now the Whig Secretary of State for Foreign Affairs, had co-operated as Tory Secretary at War in the work which he was now anxious to dissolve. As regards the Treaty of Vienna, this division of Holland and Belgium was, no doubt, a breach of that compact; but a treaty can be only binding when taken as a whole, and this breach of it was justified by the breach of one of its terms made by the King of Holland in assuming to himself powers which had been expressly taken out of his hands by the Treaty. This, however, was understood much less accurately by those out of office than by those in, and Lord Palmerston no doubt became more hot in his own defence the more he was attacked by his opponents.

We have his correspondence respecting the affairs of Belgium with Lord Granville, our Ambassador at Paris, and it is interesting to see how speedily and how warmly he takes up the Belgian question. An Englishman reading this should of course remember that Lord Palmerston was an English Minister, filled with English convictions at the moment, and that he (the reader) will of course only get the English view. But the letters do leave the impression that the English Minister only wanted what was just; and our history tells us that his views have been carried out, and that the measure, as directed by him, has been pre-eminently successful. But there is from the very first a tone of superiority in them which, though they were addressed to our own Ambassador, must have been offensive to French Ministers as they trickled through to their ears. Talleyrand, who was the French Ambassador in London, had asked that, as part of the arrangement, "Luxembourg might be given to France." But Palmerston would not hear of it, and he then writes to Lord Granville; "It may not be amiss for you to hint, upon any fitting occasion, that though we are anxious to cultivate the best understanding with France, and to be on terms of the most intimate friendship with her, yet that it is only on the supposition that she contents herself with the finest territory in Europe, and does not mean to open a new chapter of encroachment and conquest." Then we are told that, when the Luxembourg question had been given up, Talleyrand "fights like a dragon" for two Belgian fortresses,—Philippeville and Marienburg. "We had no power," says Palmerston, "to give what belongs to Belgium and not to us, and we could not, under the pretence of settling the quarrel between Holland and Belgium, proceed to plunder one of the parties, and that, too, for the benefit of one of the mediators." Talleyrand has asked questions about some increased force to our navy. "You may as well mention this conversation to Sebastiani, and take that opportunity of asking again about the Toulon ships. It is no harm, however, that the French should think that we are a little upon the alert with respect to our navy." Then there is the question, Who shall be the new King of Belgium? as to which our Minister had at first wished that a son of the King of Holland should be named. Louis Philippe wished that one of his sons should have the new throne. But Lord Palmerston will not hear of it. "I must say that if the choice falls on Nemours, and the King of the French accepts, it will be a proof that the policy of France is like an infection clinging to the walls of the dwelling, and breaking out in every successive occupant." "We are reluctant even to think of war; but if ever we are to make another effort, this is a legitimate occasion; and we find we could not submit to the placing of the Duc de Nemours on the throne of Belgium without danger to the safety, and a sacrifice of the honour of the country." "If they are straightforward in their intentions, why cannot they be so in their proceedings? Why such endless intrigues and plots, and such change of plans, all tending to the same object." Then there comes a letter, purposely written and sent in an unusual way, that it may certainly be read by Sebastiani. For it was sent through the French Foreign Office, and not by our own messengers; as to which Lord Granville observes that it will have the desired effect. "Sebastiani should really be made to understand that he must have the goodness to keep his temper, or, when it fails him, let him go to vent his ill-humour upon some other quarter, and not bestow it upon England. We are not used to being accused of making people dupes." What was Sebastiani's personal nature, we do not know. This may have made him keep his temper. But it must surely have taught him to think that our Minister was very uncivil, as he of course knew well why the letter had been sent through the French Foreign Office.

Other attempts are made by the French to get other morsels of territory into their hands, and a strong French feeling is roused in Belgium, which troubles Lord Palmerston almost as much as the French overtures made for direct French objects. A Regent, in the interests of France, was appointed during the vacancy of the throne, of whom Palmerston refuses to take any notice. "The greater part of our difficulties with the Belgians have arisen from the double diplomacy, double dealing infirmity of purpose, and want of principle in the French Government." A M. D'Arschot is sent to England as a diplomate, but Lord Palmerston refuses to see him officially. "I shall be happy to receive M. D'Arschot at my house as an individual; I cannot ask him to the office." Then he goes on. "The moment we give France a cabbage garden or a vineyard, we lose all our vantage-ground of principle; and it becomes then a mere question of degree or the relative value of the different things which, one after the other, she will demand." And he lays down a general principle, by which it will be found that he always acted. "You don't stave off war or stop demands by yielding to urgent demands, however small, from fear of war. The maxim of giving way to have an easy life will, if you follow it, lead to your having a life without a moment's ease."

At length the question as to what king should be chosen was settled by the election of Leopold to the throne of Belgium,—altogether with the good-will of Palmerston, though a Dutch Prince had been his first choice, as has been already said. But this had been done without the assent of the King of Holland; and Dutch troops marched into Belgium on one side, and French troops on the other to support Belgium. The French obtained some success, and immediately there arose the renewal of French encroachments. "As to the fortresses," says Lord Palmerston, still writing to Lord Granville, "if they expected that we were to sign a treaty with them for the destruction of those fortresses, I would tell him that I would never put my hand to such a treaty, even if the Government agreed to it." "One thing is certain,—the French must go out of Belgium, or we have a general war, and war in a given number of days." "I told him we never would agree to mix up the two questions, the departure of the French troops, and the question of the fortresses. I asked him whether his Government wished that people hereafter should believe the French Government or its word." "I have seldom seen a stronger feeling than that of the Cabinet about the question of the fortresses." "But let us stave off all these nibblings," he says in reference to a demand expressed by Prussia that Philippeville and Marienburg should be given up to France. "If once these great Powers begin to taste blood, they will never be satisfied with one bite, but will speedily devour their victim."

At last the Belgian question was settled, and a kingdom was formed, which has since remained, respected by all men, and the strongest in its circumstances among the lesser nations of the earth. To name Belgium, is to speak of good faith and constitutional well-being. The love for it which England bears was strongly evinced during the German and French war in 1870, when Bernal Osborne asked a question in the House of Commons as to the part which England would take if either party carried their armies over the frontier into Belgium. The French at that moment had been driven up into a corner at Sedan, and were compelled either to surrender or to trespass on the Belgian territory. But the question asked in the House of Commons, and the answer given, sufficed for the purpose; and no armed Frenchman and no armed German trod upon the soil which had become the Kingdom of Belgium.

Lord Palmerston had no doubt done his work well in helping the arrangement. He was disinterested throughout on the part of England, and wise, and honest, and very brave. He had allowed no foreign diplomate to hoodwink him. England, looking back at his conduct, has reason to be proud of him. But there can be no doubt that he did make himself very offensive to his French colleagues in the arrangements, and took upon himself to speak, as though he were the only honest man concerned in the work. Whether it was essential to his purpose that he should do so must now be a matter of opinion; but there can be no doubt that he made himself odious to Louis Philippe and the French Ministers, who must have looked upon him as an English bear altogether unacquainted with diplomatic courtesies. Such I think must have been the opinion held by Louis Philippe to the end. For in these years of his life it seems to have been Palmerston's business to have thwarted Louis Philippe in all his politics.

But, during the period in which the Kingdom of Belgium was being formed, the English Reform Bill was passed, a measure of such vital importance to England as almost, in English eyes, to obliterate these first struggles of Belgian infancy. But Lord Palmerston, true to his theory of political life, took but little heed of the Reform Bill. He did speak on the subject, as it was essential that he should do so; and explained how it had come to pass with him, as with others, that he had grown wiser as he had grown older. It was necessary that one, who had come into power among Lord Liverpool's Tories, should defend his vote by such an argument. But there is nothing to make us think that his heart was with the Reformers. Indeed, as long as he remained at the Foreign Office his heart was with foreign affairs. And though, as a member of a Cabinet, he was bound to support that Cabinet's measures, I should doubt whether he asked many questions on the subject. His heart was then in Belgium, and in the Quadruple Alliance for establishing free institutions in Spain and Portugal, and afterwards in creating the kingdom of Greece, and in endeavouring to stop the abominable iniquities of Louis Philippe in reference to the Spanish marriages. But he supported the Reform Bill, and in consequence of his doing so,—or in consequence, rather, of his belonging to a Whig Ministry,—he lost his seat for the University of Cambridge, and, at the general election 1832, was returned to Parliament by South Hampshire, his own county.

Allusion has been made to the pride which Lord Palmerston took in the Quadruple Alliance. The Quadruple Alliance was a compact made between England, France, Spain, and Portugal, for preserving the thrones of Spain and Portugal on behalf of Isabella and Maria, and defending the two Princesses from the machinations of their uncles, Don Carlos and Don Miguel. That the two Princesses were the legitimate heirs to the thrones need not now, specially in England, be more than stated. But the collateral object was to ensure freedom under the rule of the two Queens, instead of despotism, with all its bitterness, under the two Kings. That at least was Lord Palmerston's object; though, when we come to the story of the Spanish marriages, we shall find that Louis Philippe had a further object of his own. For some account of the kind of misery to be looked for under Don

Miguel, to whom Palmerston was specially hostile, I may refer my readers to an article in the *Edinburgh Review* of September, 1831, on the condition of Portugal.

In looking back at Lord Palmerston's career, and the entire success of his political life, we have to own that it was due to the teaching, or rather to the genius, of Mr. Canning. He had fallen into Mr. Canning's hands, and though without that fine intellect which would have enabled him to imitate the lessons which he had so learned, he was quick enough to perceive their merit, and wise enough to follow them, whether he were called Whig or Tory. Canning died, and in carrying out his lessons Palmerston had become a member of Lord Grey's Cabinet. It was not much to him whether men called him Whig or Tory. But he saw the wisdom of going still on; and whether he were Member for the University which demanded a Tory to represent it, or for his own county, which afterwards in turn again repudiated him, or for the borough of Tiverton, where he could be one or the other, he remained always true to the precepts of the school which he had adopted. "A Tory Government," he says, writing to his brother, in June, 1833, "is an utter impossibility in the present state of the public feeling; the country would not stand it." Then he goes on to speak of what he and the Cabinet had just done for the abolition of slavery. "To be sure, we give the West Indians a tolerably good compensation. I really believe that the twenty millions which are to be voted for them are about the whole value of all the estates at the present market price; so that they will receive nearly the value of their estates, and keep their estates into the bargain. I must say it is a splendid instance of generosity and justice, unexampled in the history of the world, to see a nation (for it is the national will, and not merely the resolve of the Government or the Parliament) emancipate seven hundred and fifty thousand slaves, and pay twenty millions sterling to their owners as compensation for the loss they will sustain. People sometimes are greatly generous at the expense of others, but it is not often that men are found to pay so high a price for the luxury of doing a noble action."

"Some persons on the Continent want to have it supposed that the English are so bent upon economy and retrenchment that no provocation or injury would rouse them to incur the expense of another war. This vote of so large a sum for the satisfaction of a principle ought to show those persons that it would not be safe to rely too much upon their calculation." In this he takes great pride to himself; but it is a pride in the glory of his country; and it is exhibited in private letters in which an absence of reticence is not unbecoming.

Some time previous to this he had shown the same determined spirit. Writing to our Minister in Spain in March, 1831, he says, "It is well known that every river on the coast of Africa, where slaves are obtained, still swarms with slave ships, bearing openly the flag of Spain; while vessel after vessel sails for that coast from the Havannah, returns laden with these slaves, of whom even the number on board is probably known, lands them unmolested at the back of the island of Cuba, re-enters the port of the Havannah in ballast, and is again fitted up, rapidly and without impediment, for a fresh expedition in this prohibited traffic."

In 1834 the Slave Commissioner, at Sierra Leone, writes to him on the subject. "The traffic under the Portuguese flag, which for years past had been almost unheard of, appears now to be carried on to as great an extent as it was before Brazil ceased to belong to Portugal." In the same year Mr. Macleay, our British Commissioner at the Havannah, complains to him on the same subject,—of the trade as carried on under the new Captain-General of Cuba. From this we may see that our Foreign Minister found ample matters on which to write to the servants of other Crowns so as to make himself enemies. It is not to be doubted but that he did write with all the pertinacity of purpose which is apt to be odious to people who entertain opinions opposed to those who exercise it.

The above references have been taken from the *Quarterly Review* of December, 1835. If we turn to the July number of the *Edinburgh Review* for 1836, we shall find him and the slave trade spoken of in the same spirit; but the tone is so hearty that I will venture to quote the passage:—"Every Power in Europe has acknowledged that a solemn obligation is upon them to contribute to the abolition of the accursed traffic in our fellow creatures. Each also admits that their formal declaration to that effect, made more than twenty years ago, has to this hour been fruitless, and the pledges then given to use every means in the power of each to effect it, still unredeemed. The frivolous pretexts which have been advanced by some for not adopting the only means which experience has shown to be effectual, require only to be refuted, and the object to be sincerely and heartily pursued by us, and complete success cannot be far distant. We have abundant evidence before us that no exertions will be wanting on the part of Lord Palmerston. His urgent remonstrances and representations have been poured into every country of the civilized world. His tone has been firm and decisive when our slave treaties have been infringed. He has used argument and persuasion where as yet there had been no obligation. After a careful perusal of the documents before us, we hesitate not to say that his zealous, consistent, and able advocacy of this great cause, while it tends to raise his country high among nations for enlightened humanity and for moral worth, will constitute, next to the preservation of peace, his worthiest title to a lasting reputation."

His work is incessant, and he can hardly allow himself a few days of holiday when the Session is over. "I may then manage to get down to Broadlands for a week, and I long for a little rest." At the end of the year he joins a shooting party, but is not able "to get out of town for more than four days at a time. I had three days shooting at Woburn last week, and pretty good sport. An official party, Grey, Brougham, Lansdowne (now combatants), Althorp, Melbourne, Ripon, Graham, John Russell, Auckland, Ellice, myself, young Ellice and Lord Charles Russell, were the sharpshooters." We see from the names above given, that he had now fallen entirely among the Whigs; for Sir James Graham was then a Whig. "I must say that this reformed House of Commons is growing to be wonderfully like its predecessors; impatient of fools, intolerant of blackguards." It is much the same thing at present, though now the blackguards have to be tolerated. Then he speaks exultingly of the Quadruple Alliance between England, France, Spain and Portugal for the expulsion of Carlos and Miguel. He speaks almost boastingly of his own power. "I carried it through the Cabinet by a *coup de main*, taking them by surprise, and not leaving them time to make objections." This is the spirit in which he looks at all his own doings as Minister for Foreign Affairs, and though we may be angry at the boasting, we cannot but acknowledge that it was this spirit which kept him up. Then we have him for a week down in Hampshire among his race-horses. But his papers follow him. "I was a week at Broadlands entirely by myself, working all day, and almost every day, at F. O. boxes and Holmes's accounts for the last three years, which I had not before been able to look at; they were all right, however." After this he tells us of that wicked Thresher who only provided sixteen pheasants for five guns to kill in Yew Tree. After that he speaks again of the Quadruple Alliance, and again exults. "This treaty was a capital hit, and all my own doing." Mr. Ashley, however, adds that "this treaty was a full completion of Mr. Canning's policy."

❑❑❑

CHAPTER V

Palmerston as Foreign Secretary, April, 1835, to August, 1841

WHY Lord Grey abandoned the Government in 1834, and why he refused to come back again either in 1834 or in 1835, is a question in English politics which it is difficult to answer. That it was occasioned, as Lord Palmerston says, by Mr. O'Connell and the Irish Coercion Act may be true; but why it should have been occasioned thereby is another question. In the summer of 1834 the Government went out with Lord Grey at its head, and came back with Lord Melbourne instead of Lord Grey. The world was astonished when it saw how good a Prime Minister it had in Lord Melbourne, and how sufficiently clever he was for all the purposes of his position; and the old-fashioned world has hardly yet got over its astonishment as it looks back on the strong and adequate conduct of William Lamb in that position. In July, 1834, the King chose him for the office, and Lord Palmerston, of course, remained with him. But in November, 1834, the Tories came in. "We are all out," says Lord Palmerston to his brother. "Turned out neck and crop. Wellington is Prime Minister, and we give up the seals, etc., to-morrow at St. James's at two. I am told Ellenborough succeeds me. The Speaker takes the Home Office, *ad interim*, and till Peel returns from Italy." Then he adds, "This attempt to re-install the Tories cannot possibly last. The country will not stand it. The House of Commons will not bear it."

This change had been brought about by the death of Lord Spencer, whose eldest son, Lord Althorp, became a peer, and could no longer lead the House of Commons. There was a project to make Lord Palmerston leader, and it was a position for which he afterwards proved himself to be pre-eminently fitted. But King William took advantage of the accident of Lord Althorp's peerage, and was carried by his royal instincts into the arms of the Duke of Wellington and Sir Robert Peel. This King has always borne the character of being a true Liberal. The Reform Bill was passed in his days, and a Tory minister and Tory principles were for a time impossible. But for a few months, when Lord Grey had gone, and Lord Althorp had been removed from the House of Commons, he went back to Toryism, as it was surely natural that a king should do. But here must be given an extract from a kindly letter which the King wrote to Lord Palmerston on his leaving office, which is inserted for the purpose of showing that though the Foreign Secretary had no doubt made himself disagreeable to the King of the French and to his servants, he had contrived to make himself pleasant to his own sovereign. "His Majesty has, at all times, derived satisfaction from the free and unreserved character of Viscount Palmerston's official intercourse with him, and from the anxiety which he has shown to afford to him upon every matter the most ample information, and all the explanation which he could possibly require, and His Majesty assures Lord Palmerston that he will always take a constant interest in his welfare and happiness.

"WILLIAM R."

But though the Tories were strong in hope, and Sir Robert Peel had hurried back from Italy very fast,—but hardly fast enough to satisfy the longings of his party,—they were not destined to remain in power. On April 21, 1835, he once more writes to his brother from the Foreign Office, "Here I am again at my old work." But at the general election he had lost his seat for South Hampshire, the county having a county's dislike to a Whig member. Lord Palmerston had, however, found a seat at Tiverton, which he kept till he died. We are told that at this period he nearly slipped out of official life, having in truth but few strong ties by which he was bound to other men. Some asked themselves the question, why was he there,—he who had so lately been a Tory, and had done so little for his adopted party? For his work had been office work, diplomatic work, silent work, done by the pen rather than by the tongue, and had not recommended itself to the Radicals. The Foreign Office was a place of great power, and very desirable. Why should it not be given to some man who had made himself hot with the heat of the battle of Reform? And when the time came that he was without a seat it might have been easy to pass him over. He did not belong to any great Whig ducal house, nor had he put himself forward as a popular speaker. But he had his eyes wide open, and knew well how to say a word in season. And he selected his special friends with judgment. Lord Melbourne was his friend, and Lord Melbourne reinstated him at the Foreign Office.

On his reappointment, he expressed an opinion to his brother, the truth of which every Englishman will feel. "The truth is that English interests continue the same, let who will be in office, and that upon leading principles and great measures men of both sides, when they come to act dispassionately and with responsibility upon them, will be found acting very much alike." The meaning of this is that an English statesman cannot dare to be other than honest. The right thing to do must be the right thing, whether Lord Aberdeen or Lord Palmerston be in power. When some vital question comes up as to the spreading or confining the British Empire in India, and adding a new nation to our responsibilities, then there may be a difference in policy, and one set of Ministers may fail to carry out the projects of their predecessors. But in the ordinary affairs of European politics, in which clear-seeing eyes may certainly discern what honesty demands, Whigs and Tories, Liberals and Conservatives, will be found "acting very much alike."

It was now that Lord Palmerston obtained the sanction of the Cabinet for the British Legion in Spain. It was intended to assist Queen Isabella in opposing the priests and the Inquisition. It no doubt did have that effect, though it was not altogether a success, and Sir de Lacy Evans, at the head of the Legion, was so badly handled as to make the matter appear a fitting subject for a Parliamentary attack on Lord Palmerston. This was done with great vigour and, through a debate which lasted for three nights, it was almost doubtful which way the majority might decide. Towards the end of it Lord Palmerston spoke, and proved that the silence which was usual to him did not come from want of capacity to speak, or want of fire in speaking when the subject seemed to justify it. The speech is thus described by Mr. Edward Ellice; "It is, however, useless to say any more of it than that Palmerston has made so admirable a speech in every respect as completely to have gained the House, and to have re-established himself entirely in their good opinion, if there was a question of his having lost it in some quarters. He spoke for three hours; and I never heard a more able, vigorous, or successful defence of the foreign policy of a Government, or war better or more happily and fearlessly carried into the enemy's quarters." And we are told that the House was riotous with cheering throughout. When it divided, however, there was a majority of no more than thirty-six among five hundred and twenty members.

In reading the letters from Lord Palmerston to his brother and to Lord Granville, we cannot but feel sometimes that they were written with a view to the public. They contain sententious morsels of didactic wisdom, which would not have not been put there in the hurry of private correspondence unless they had been intended for other eyes. "When two of the most powerful maritime nations accept us as mediators upon a point of national honour, it is clear that they must think that we have not forfeited our own." "England," he says, "is to be as full of railways as a ploughed field is of furrows, but the crop they will bear is more doubtful." "The nobles both in Spain and Portugal are the most incapable part of the nation, and therefore a remodelling of the Upper Chambers in both countries seems a reasonable thing." "No empire is likely to fall to pieces if left to itself, and if no kind neighbours forcibly tear it to pieces." "Half the wrong conclusions at which mankind arrive are leached by the abuse of metaphors." And we do not always feel that he is right. He gets a little out of his element when he attempts to draw the conclusions at which he arrives. But when he tells of a fact, and of his conclusion from that, he is always correct. In reference to the King's speech in January, 1837, he says: "On Foreign affairs we shall say little, and especially not a word about France or French Alliance. We can say nothing in their praise, and therefore silence is the most complimentary thing we can bestow upon them." At this period we certainly could have said nothing complimentary respecting France, as the Spanish marriages were coming on, and the preparations for the Spanish marriages were being made.

In 1837 King William died, and the present Sovereign came to the throne. She was then but eighteen years old, but immediately showed her fitness for her high office. "The Queen went through her task to-day with great dignity and self-possession," Lord Palmerston says, writing to Lord Granville. "One saw she felt much inward emotion; but it was fully controlled. Her articulation was peculiarly good; her voice remarkably pleasing." "They," the foreign Ministers, "were introduced one by one. Nothing could be better than her manner of receiving them; it is easy, and dignified, and gracious." "There will be lots of extra ambassadors, and shoals of princes, at our coronation. Heaven knows what we shall do with them, or how and where they will find lodging. They will be disappointed, both as to the effect they will themselves produce, and as to the splendour of the ceremony they come to witness. State coaches, fine liveries, and gilt harness make no sensation in London, except among coachmakers and stablemen." And then he adds: "I do not think that marriage has yet entered the Queen's head; perhaps some of her visitors may inspire her with the idea; but after being used to agreeable and well-informed Englishmen, I fear she will not find a foreign prince to her liking." As to the foreign prince, however, Palmerston proved himself to have been absolutely wrong.

In 1838 and 1839 Mehemet Ali was a great man. He had obtained for himself the Pashalic of Egypt and the Dominion of Syria. Not content with that, he desired further influence in European Turkey; and had probably conceived in his brain the idea of first upsetting, and then occupying the throne of the Sultan. Though in this he would not have succeeded, as the powers were too strong for him, he would probably have enabled the Emperor of Russia to have taken possession of Constantinople, as the protector of the Turk, but for the zeal and readiness of the English. It must not be told here how Sir Charles Napier,—Don Carlos de Ponza, as Lord Palmerston called him,—put an end to this dream by taking first Sidon, and then Acre, and created that enthusiasm in the mind of Palmerston which afterwards led to the unfortunate dinner at the Reform Club, to the taking of Bomarsund in lieu of Cronstadt, and resulted at last in the bitterness of the Admiral's parliamentary attacks on his old friends when the Crimean war was over. It is useless now to look back and to suggest what would have happened had things been allowed to take another course. But if Russia had then been the protector of Turkey instead of England, the latter campaign, if fought at all, would have taken place nearer to the more hospitable regions of Middle Europe than the Crimea. As it was, Mehemet Ali was stopped, and Turkey was defended, and Russia for awhile kept in its place, I must not say by the zeal of Lord Palmerston,—because it would be going too far to give to him the entire credit of doing what England did,—but with his co-operation and in conformity with his councils. It was at the time presumed that Mehemet Ali was struggling for supreme power, in conformity with French tactics; or, in other words, that France was seeking to obtain the upper hand in Egypt. We were then awake to the necessity of maintaining for ourselves a way through Egypt to India. This we were bound to do for the preservation of our Indian Empire, and should probably have done it under any circumstances; but Lord Palmerston took so prominent a part in the matter that it is necessary to follow him in his eagerness for a few pages.

There were three parties with whom he had to carry on the contest; and among the three the first was that which occasioned him the least trouble. They were Mehemet Ali himself, the King of the French, and the opposing members of our own Cabinet. It was comparatively easy to dispose of Mehemet Ali, with the assistance of Sir Charles Napier; but Louis Philippe was an antagonist with whom it was much more difficult to deal. Palmerston put no trust in Louis Philippe, regarding him from first to last as an enemy to English practices and English aspirations; but neither was he afraid of Louis Philippe and his Minister. He was afraid of some among his own colleagues, who could only with great difficulty be got to act with him in opposition to French counsels. He writes as follows to Lord Granville; "Let the French say what they like, they cannot go to war with the four Powers in support of Mehemet Ali. Would they hazard a naval war for such an object? Where are they to find ships to equal or to contend with the British navy alone, leaving out the Russian navy, which in such case would join us? What would become of Algiers if they were at war with a Power superior to France at sea? Would they risk a Continental war? And for what? Could they help Mehemet Ali by marching to the Rhine? And would they not be driven back as fast as they went? It is impossible. The French may talk big, but they cannot make war for such a cause. It would be very unwise to underrate the force of France and the evils of a war with her in a case in which she had national interest and a just cause; but it would be equally inexpedient to be daunted by big words and empty vapouring in a case in which a calm view of things ought to convince one that France alone would be the sufferer by a war hastily, capriciously, and unjustly undertaken by herself." Thiers and Guizot were at this time the chief advisers of Louis Philippe, M. Guizot having become the French Ambassador in London. But Lord Palmerston believed not much in any of the three. "The truth is," he says, "however reluctantly one may avow the conviction, that Louis Philippe is a man in whom no solid trust can be reposed. However, there he is, and we call him our ally; only we ought to be enlightened by experience and not to attach to his assertions or professions any greater value than really belongs to them; more especially when, as in the case of Egypt, his words are not only at variance with his conduct, but even inconsistent with each other. The Cabinet have determined that we must without delay bring the French to a clear and definite arrangement about their fleet." Austria, Prussia, and Russia were willing to act with us, but were not willing to take a part so active as that which Palmerston desired on the part of England.

But it was necessary to act in co-operation with these Powers, and it was found very difficult to obtain the accord of the entire British Cabinet. In consequence of this we find him writing to Lord Melbourne on the 5th of July, 1840, and offering to resign his post

"The difference of opinion which seems to exist between myself and some members of the Cabinet upon the Turkish question, has led me, upon full consideration, to the conviction that it is a duty which I owe to myself and to my colleagues to relieve you and others from the necessity of deciding between my views and those of other members of the Cabinet on these matters, by placing, as I now do, my office at your disposal. My opinion upon this question is distinct and unqualified. I think that the object to be attained is of the utmost importance for the interests of England, for the preservation of the balance of power, and for the maintenance of peace in Europe. I find the three Powers entirely prepared to concur in the views which I entertain on this matter if these views should be the views of the British Government. I can feel no doubt that the four Powers, acting in union with, and in support of the Sultan, are perfectly able to carry those views into effect; and I think that the commercial and political interests of Great Britain, the honour and dignity of the country, good faith towards the Sultan, and sound views of European policy, all require that we should adopt such a course. If we draw back, and shrink from a co-operation with Austria, Russia, and Prussia in this matter, because France stands aloof and will not join, we shall place this country in the degraded position of being held in leading-strings by France, and shall virtually acknowledge that, even when supported by the other three Powers of the Continent, we dare embark in no system of policy in opposition to the will of France, and consider her positive concurrence as a necessary condition for our action. The ultimate results of such a decision will be the practical division of the Turkish Empire into two separate and independent states, whereof one will be the dependency of France, and the other a satellite of Russia; and in both of which our political influence will be annulled, and our commercial interests will be sacrificed; and this dismemberment will inevitably give rise to local struggles and conflicts which will involve the Powers of Europe in most serious disputes." "Twice my opinion on these affairs has been overruled by the Cabinet, and twice the policy which I recommended has been set aside. First, in 1833, when the Sultan sent to ask our aid before Mehemet Ali had made any material progress in Syria, and when

Russia expressed her wish that we should assist the Sultan,—saying, however, that if we did not, she would. Secondly, in 1835, when France was ready to have united with us in a treaty with the Sultan for the maintenance of the integrity of his empire." "We have now arrived at a third crisis, when the resolution of the British Cabinet will exercise a deciding influence upon future events; but this time the danger is more apparent and undisguised, and the remedy is more complete and within our reach. The matter to be dealt with belongs to my department, and I should be held in a peculiar degree personally responsible for the consequences of any course which I might undertake to conduct. I am sure, therefore, that you cannot wonder that I should decline to be the instrument for carrying out a policy which I disapprove, and that I should consequently take the step which I have stated in the beginning of this letter."

Lord Melbourne, however, induced him to withdraw his resignation, assuring him that it would involve the dissolution of the Government. "And," he added, "how another is to be formed in the present state of parties and opinions I see not." The Cabinet yielded, and Lord Palmerston had his way, as he usually did have, by a singular mixture of undaunted pluck and rectitude of purpose. I do not venture to assert that in this Turkish question Lord Palmerston did that which the welfare of the East of Europe certainly demanded. It is useless now to think whether the Bulgarian horrors might have been avoided in 1876 had not Lord Palmerston supported the Sultan in 1840, as it is also to argue that England could not have maintained her power in Europe and her hold over Egypt had she not then supported Turkey. Considerations of matters so intricate are too difficult for a little book such as this, however fitting they may be for deeper and longer volumes. My business is here to explain the nature of the conduct and character of Lord Palmerston. And when I speak of his rectitude of purpose I allude rather to his motives than to his actions. To do the best he could for English interests, and to do that best in an honest and manly manner, was his object; and the world may therefore give him credit for rectitude of purpose. The world must give him credit also for positive success.

Just when Palmerston was offering to resign his seat in the Cabinet, meaning to show thereby that his power of carrying his own views in the Government was not to be contested seriously, though questions concerning it might be raised, a whole series of pamphlets appeared against him, in which he was accused of selling his own country to Russia. These charges came chiefly from one Mr. Urquhart, who had been put into the Civil Service by Lord Palmerston himself, and had since filled himself with an idea that his former employer had become false to his country. Mr. Urquhart's furor was so like madness that it would not be here mentioned, were it not worth our while to spend a page in showing the kind of things which were published at the time. There was a Mr. Doubleday, who, at a meeting at Newcastle, spoke as follows;—"I hereby declare my conviction that Lord Palmerston is a traitor, and ought to be impeached; and, if found guilty before a tribunal of his country, his head ought to roll upon the scaffold!" "I happen to know that this man was, a few years ago, as poor as a person called a lord could well be conceived to be,—that he was hunted about, and had half a dozen executions in his house at once,—and now, without any visible cause, without any visible means of making a better livelihood, this man has suddenly become rich, has paid all his debts, and is living upon the fat of the land. What rational conclusion can one come to but that he is enabled to do this by means of Russian gold?" For these calumnies there is not a tittle of excuse. There was not a word of truth in them. We are sometimes inclined to think that bitterness of speech against public men has now attained a worse acrimony than it ever did. But when we look back at some of these speeches against Lord Palmerston, we shall see that it is not so.

In 1839, an accusation had been made against Lord Palmerston, alleging that in dealing with foreign affairs he was too ready to sacrifice British interests, being the reverse of the medal as it was afterwards exhibited, in which he was shown as offending all foreigners by his arrogance in asserting every thing British. To this latter accusation he was probably open;—but the other was brought against him also, and then he defended himself: "In the outset, I must deny the charge made personally against myself, and against the Government to which

I belong, of an identification with the interests of other nations. I venture to say that never was there an Administration that paid more attention to the commercial interests of this country. And this I will add, that much as I feel the importance of the alliance of this country with other Powers, and much as I wish to perpetuate such alliances, and to endeavour to render other nations as friendly as possible with this, I am satisfied that the interest of England is the Polar star,—the guiding principle of the conduct of the Government." Here, no doubt, he declared the purpose and the practice of his life;—the practice, by adhering to which he so nearly became shipwrecked, but succeeded in obtaining that special attachment which is felt for his name among Englishmen generally.

On the 13th of July, 1840, he continued the correspondence with his brother William, the treaty with Austria, Prussia, and Russia, for restraining Mehemet Ali, being dated on the subsequent 15th. He gives the particulars of the treaty which, had it been accepted by Mehemet, would have left Syria in his hands for life. But it was not accepted, and Syria was consequently taken away by the victories of Sidon and Acre. But Lord Palmerston, in the same letter, goes on to other subjects. The Queen had now been married, and a child is to be born. "Prince Albert is to be sole Regent during the confinement of the Queen, and if any misfortune were to happen during the minority of the heir to the throne, or rather of the infant sovereign, there is already a Bill in force to provide for the Regency till the arrival of Ernest, if, as a signal punishment for the sins of the nation, he were to come to the throne of England." This was Ernest, the Duke of Cumberland, as well as King of Hanover. Then, in the easy tone of fraternal conversation, he rushes on to another matter.

"My Priam filly, three-year old, out of Gallopade's dam, has won the only two races she has started for; one at Stockbridge, and the Queen's Plate at Guildford; and she may win a stake this week at Southampton."

We must here for awhile go back, before we finish the story of Mehemet Ali, to two circumstances, one of which had a considerable interest among the political quidnuncs of the day, and the other a more lasting influence on the life of Lord Palmerston himself. In the spring of 1839 the Government was nearly beaten on the question of the Jamaica Constitution, having been supported by a majority of only five. They resigned in consequence, and Sir Robert Peel, having been desired to form a Government, broke down under the difficulties imposed upon him in reference to the ladies of the household. "They insisted on the removal of the Ladies of the Bedchamber. The Queen declared she would not submit to it; that it would be too painful and affronting to her; that those ladies have no seats in Parliament; that the object in view in dismissing them was to separate her from everybody in whom she could trust, and to surround her with political spies, if not with personal enemies." "The Queen, alone and unadvised, stood firm against all these assaults, showed a presence of mind, a firmness, a discrimination, far beyond her years." "We shall, of course, stand by the Queen, and support her against this offensive condition which the Tories wanted to impose upon her, and which her youth and isolated condition ought to have protected her from."

In all this Lord Palmerston takes the part of his Cabinet against Sir Robert Peel's, with all the eagerness of a partisan, and did, no doubt, feel as he wrote. But it was thought at the time that there was much to be said for Sir Robert's view of the case, and that however well he might have been able to contest political questions with a Whig Cabinet, he could not have done so with any chance of success against the wives and sisters of Whig Ministers. The ladies, however, won the battle, and the Whigs patched up their majority again, sufficiently to enable them to go on. The other event was the marriage of Lord Palmerston with the Countess Cowper, which took place on December 11, 1839. This lady, who had been left a widow in June, 1837, was sister to Lord Melbourne. She immediately took the name of her second husband, though in a rank inferior to that which she at the time enjoyed, and is still remembered as the most popular woman in London. She brought to her husband a considerable accession of fortune, and, among other things, Brocket Hall, in Hertfordshire, which had been the seat of her brother, and in which he died, and in which Lord Palmerston, another Prime Minister, was fated to die also. Lord Palmerston, we may imagine, had but few things to regret in the world; but this marriage, which he did not achieve till he had reached the ripe age of fifty-five, certainly was not one of them.

Now we must go back and finish the story of Mehemet Ali, as far as Lord Palmerston is concerned with it, and also the record of his doings as Foreign Secretary up to the year 1841. All through 1840 we find him carrying on the battle. "Guizot has looked as cross as the devil for the last few days," he says in one of his letters; "and, indeed, on Sunday, when he dined here, he could scarcely keep up the outward appearances of civility." And then writing still to Mr. Bulwer, who was acting as Ambassador in Paris, "If Thiers should again hold to you the language of menace, however indistinctly and vaguely shadowed out, pray retort upon him to the full extent of what he may say to you; and with that skill of language which I know you to be master of, convey to him, in the most friendly and inoffensive manner possible, that if France throws down the gauntlet we shall not refuse to pick it up; and that if she begins a war she will to a certainty lose her ships, colonies, and commerce, before she sees the end of it; that her army of Algiers will cease to give her anxiety; and that Mehemet Ali will just be chucked into the Nile." "Really Thiers must think us wonderful simpletons to be thus bamboozled."

The reader can tell, without any reference to Lord Palmerston's private notes, those despatches of which he has intended that the very spirit, if not the language, shall be made known to his French antagonist. Convey to him in the "most friendly and inoffensive manner possible that if France throws down the gauntlet we shall not refuse to pick it up!" What other Minister ever wrote in language made so monstrously uncivil by its mock civility? But his anger is not only against France and Frenchmen, but also against certain Englishmen whom he does not name, but who, we are left to believe, sat in the same Cabinet with himself, or formed part of the same administration. "I must say I never in my life was more disgusted with anything than I have been by the conduct of certain parties,—useless now to name,—in all this affair." He is supposed here to have alluded specially to Lord Holland, who had opposed him in the Cabinet. Lord Holland died shortly afterwards, and then Lord Palmerston had nothing to say of him but what was good and affectionate. Further on he writes to Lord Granville, who had returned to Paris by October: "Pray go to the King immediately, and say you are instructed to deprecate in the most friendly, but at the same time the most earnest, manner, steps which we hear are under consideration, and which, if taken, would either make war inevitable, or at least render the continuation or resumption (if they have ceased) of friendly relations a matter of the utmost difficulty."

Palmerston goes on doggedly with his projects, and does not cease to boast as to his progress. Still writing to Lord Granville, he says, on 23rd October, 1840; "It is plain that we have as good as driven Mehemet Ali out of the whole of Syria." "Indeed, I have good reason to believe, by information I have received from Paris, that Mehemet has sent to Thiers to beg he would make the best terms he could for him." "Louis Philippe seems to have held to you the same language which Flahault and Guizot held while here, namely, that it is necessary, in order to assist the King to maintain peace and keep down the war party, that we should make to the entreaties of the King those concessions which we have refused to the threats of Thiers. But this is quite impossible, and you cannot too soon or too strongly explain it to all parties concerned." "All Frenchmen want to encroach and extend their territorial possessions at the expense of other nations; and they all feel, what the *National* has often said, that an alliance with England is a bar to such projects." "It is a misfortune to Europe that the national character of a great and powerful people, placed in the centre of Europe, should be such as it is." And on the 15th of November he says; "Rémusat has let the cat out of the bag, by declaring that France, in protecting Mehemet Ali, meant to establish a new second-rate maritime power in the Mediterranean, whose fleet might unite with that of France, for the purpose of serving as a counterpoise to that of England." And on the 26th: "Mehemet is the subject of the Sultan, and nothing more, and never can or will be anything more." "I am very sorry to find that M. Guizot is still hankering after Mehemet Ali, and clinging to the broken-down policy of Thiers. Pray communicate the substance of this letter to M. Guizot." And then comes the final blast of the trumpet. "My dear Granville,—This day has brought us a flight of good news; Mehemet's submission"—together with other good news from foreign parts. "The general result"—and here I quote Mr. Ashley's words—"of this long but successful contest over Eastern affairs, was to produce the same respect for the names of Palmerston and England in the East as had been already produced in Europe. Those names were whispered in the tents of the Arabs with fear and reverence."

But what was felt in England as to these matters is, we should say, of higher moment in regard to our Minister's reputation. The outspoken words of Englishmen are of more avail than the whisperings of Arabs. The writers of the *Quarterly* and the *Edinburgh* are supposed, at any rate, to write with their eyes open. But here we find that each party fights manfully, simply on its own side. Writing in April, 1837, the *Quarterly* thus expresses itself; "The tinkering our Constitution has undergone at the hands of Whig-Radical Ministers has certainly not tended to elevate it in the estimation of foreigners, and Lord Palmerston's foreign policy bids fair to bring the English flag into downright contempt from one end of Europe to the other." So much for the Tory view of the years with which we have been dealing. When we turn to the July number of the *Edinburgh* for 1840, we find the Whig idea of our foreign politics thus given: "It was the moral influence of the policy of England at this period, which preserved Europe in a state of tranquillity, and maintained that equipoise on which every hope of peace depended." Perhaps, after all, when party feelings ran so high at home—and still run so high—the greater dependence may be placed on the Arab whisperings. No doubt a knowledge of the policy of the world at large is necessary to determine the respect or contempt for England which was felt when Lord Palmerston was at the Foreign Office. But I doubt whether any Tory can hesitate on the matter; and my conviction is the stronger seeing that the charge now made against Lord Palmerston is, not that he showed a tendency to bully, but that he was so efficacious in bullying.

❑❑❑

CHAPTER VI

Palmerston Out of Office, August, 1841, To July, 1846.

IN the summer of 1845 Lord Melbourne went out of office, never to come back again, and Lord Palmerston, of course, went with him, having still before him twenty-four years of active official life. Lord Melbourne was only six years his senior, but he died at Brocket Hall in 1848. Lord Melbourne and Lord Palmerston had remained together since 1827, when Lord Melbourne, as William Lamb, was Secretary for Ireland. They had been united in a peculiar manner, each trusting the other, and believing in each other, not simply as Cabinet Ministers, but as friends whose ideas in politics were the same. Though Whig statesmen, they were at heart Conservatives. They afterwards became brothers-in-law. Lord Melbourne's name occurs again in Lord Palmerston's letters, but it is only in reference to the late Prime Minister's illness. Lord Palmerston was too intent on public life to allow him a moment in which to hark back upon what was past I think it is the case that a statesman generally dies out of the memory of his contemporaries very quickly. Some savour of Palmerston and Peel does remain; but almost none of Melbourne and Aberdeen. Soon there will be but little of Disraeli.

The Whigs had been in office long enough for the country, which always desires a change after a period of four or five, or perhaps seven or eight years. Lord John Russell and Lord Palmerston were undoubtedly popular in the House of Commons, of which Lord John was probably a more capable leader than any who have lived during the last half century, unless it be Lord Palmerston himself. But the Ministry had become weak, and, as Lord Palmerston said, "the Tories were anxious to turn them out." He did not add, as he might have done, that the Whigs were as anxious to turn out the Tories whenever the Tories were in. *C'la va sans dire*, we may say of both; nor would the Liberals and Conservatives of to-day be worthy of their name unless as much could be predicated of them. On this occasion a direct vote of want of confidence was brought, and the House was so equally divided that there was a majority of one against the Government. Then they dissolved Parliament, and in the new House the Tories had a majority of seventy-two. Upon this the Whigs, of course, retired.

On going out of office Palmerston seems to have been specially perturbed, because he was unable to sign, as one of the plenipotentiaries, the new Slave Trade commission. This was postponed till it was necessary that the signature should be given by Lord Aberdeen, who was his successor, and he attributes the delay to wilful spite on the part of Guizot, with whom, as will have been seen, he had been constantly at loggerheads. "It is very shabby of Guizot to endeavour to shirk this, in order to sign with Aberdeen a treaty which I have been hammering at this four years." That he should have felt this may be natural; but the mention of the grievance as a thing to be complained of even to such a friend as Sir Henry Bulwer, was hardly worth his while. From the summer of 1841 to the summer of 1846 Lord Palmerston remained for five years in Opposition, and during that period we must pass over his career somewhat quickly, because he was not a man who seems to have taken upon himself the hot and eager work of turning out Administrations, unless when, as was subsequently the case, he had to stand up in the ring, and have one lusty round with his old friend, John Russell. When personally attacked, he would hit back with all his strength, but he never seems to have felt rancour afterwards, and on the occasion to which allusion has been made, he returned almost at once into amicable relations with his old friend.

He did, however, as soon as he was out of power, attack Lord Stanley, who, since he had come into office, had spoken more than once on Foreign affairs, although that department was not peculiarly his own. And at this period of his life Lord Palmerston seems to have gone back to that system of making premeditated speeches, which is the common lot of all leading politicians; though it was one which he had altogether refused to adopt during the years that he had been at the Foreign Office. Nor had he complied with it while at the War Office. Now he did make his attacks, not with venom indeed, but with some sharpness. "I must say that the noble Lord's charge shows a great want of information on his part, as to the state of our foreign relations. It may be that the noble Lord and his colleagues have been too busily occupied in their own departments to have leisure to ransack the archives of the Foreign Office to know what passed in our time; but then, really, they who are so wholly uninformed ought not to make such positive assertions. But the noble Lord's attack upon me and my colleagues is an instance, not only of great want of information, but also of the grossest ingratitude. So far from having left embarrassments to our successors, we have bequeathed to them facilities. Why, what have they been doing since they came into office? They have been living upon our leavings. They have been subsisting upon the broken victuals which they found upon our table. They are like a band of men who have made a forcible entrance into a dwelling, and who sit down and carouse upon the provision they found in the larder." The accusation is one which has always been made, and always will be made, by progressive against stationary politicians. We all know the story of the Tory finding the Whig bathing and running away with his clothes. Of course the Conservative wishes to prevent the Liberal from being successful, and finds that he can best do so by carrying out the measures which the Liberal has proposed. Is there any man in England who has thought that Catholic Emancipation, Free Trade in corn, or Reform of Parliament has been dear to the normal Tory mind?

Lord Palmerston made his attack on Lord Stanley in the speech above quoted. Lord Stanley treasured up the grievance; and in years to come, when Palmerston was back at the Foreign Office, in 1850, had his revenge, by the studied accusation he made in the House of Lords in regard to Don Pacifico. But Don Pacifico and the circumstances of his eventful career were still in the womb of time.

He at once begins life as an idle man; and tells his brother of a series of visitings, which he has made. Then he goes on to his racing. His famous mare Ilione has come out, and he has won a stake of £1,700 with her at Newmarket;—against which, however, he acknowledges that John Day, the trainer, will send him a long bill. "Then came Holmes' accounts, which have necessarily fallen greatly into arrear." Holmes was his steward. He writes a word of criticism about the present Government; "The country will understand what they are, and find out the difference between them and us. We shall have a little comparative repose, and shall be able to attend somewhat to our own affairs."

He is still eager about the slave trade, and very busy also in abusing Guizot "The French Government have got themselves into a nice hobble about the Slave Trade Treaty. They cannot ratify without disgusting their deputies. They cannot refuse to ratify without bringing dishonour upon the Crown of France." "All this comes from Guizot's pitiful spite towards me for our success in the Syrian affair." He is said to have declared of himself that during his many years at the Foreign Office, no subject was more constantly in his thoughts than the slave trade. And now, during the period of his leisure, he dinned the matter into the ears of the House of Commons. We, who are old, can remember how urgent he was, in season and out of season, respecting the African cruisers; and how, in disregard of all criticism, he "hammered away," as he called it, so that the world should know that the slave trade had one enemy who would never yield. He never did yield; and though his service in the cause of free labour was not so palpable as that of Wilberforce and Buxton, who brought about the total abolition of slavery in the British Colonies, he did fully as much by forcing other nations into treaties, and then watching closely to see that those treaties were maintained.

In 1842, Lord Ashburton was sent to the United States with the object of establishing by treaty a boundary between them and British

America; and while he was there he had also entrusted to him the duty of making some arrangement in reference to the Right of Search. We wanted to look for Africans intended for the slave market. No doubt we could not do so on board vessels belonging to nations which had not entered into treaty with us to that effect. But we claimed the right to see whether a vessel was in truth what she called herself. But the Americans would admit no Right of Search; and Palmerston roused himself into wrath on the occasion. "Ashburton's treaty," he writes, "is very discreditable to the negotiators who concluded it, and to the Government who sanctioned it." "Our Foreign Affairs are getting into the most miserable state, and the country is fast falling from the position in which we had placed it. This Ashburton Treaty is a most disgraceful surrender to American bullying, for I cannot ever give Ashburton and the Government the credit of having been out-witted." He has already stated that "Lord Ashburton has, if possible, greater interest in America than in England." This probably was altogether incorrect. But the statement made at such a time shows the animus of the man, and the strong feeling with which he viewed anything which seemed to have a flavour of surrendering British interests.

In 1844, O'Connell was tried for conspiracy, and convicted by a Protestant jury, and was put into prison. He appealed to the House of Lords; and there, it will not perhaps be too much to say, that the matter was tried on its political, rather than on its legal bearings. There were five lords, and the three who reversed the decision of the Court below were Liberals. Palmerston continually alludes to the subject in the letters to his brother. He speaks of the trial without any violence, and almost without the expression of an opinion. When the House of Lords had decided, he wrote as follows;—"The ending of the O'Connell trial has surprised us all; but the man most surprised is Chief Justice Tindal, who, having given the opinion of the majority of the judges in the House of Lords, thought the matter settled, and set off the same night for his summer excursion. Upon arriving at Frankfort, the day before yesterday, he met Bellenden Kerr, one of our Commissioners for digesting the criminal law, who immediately made an experiment on his legal digestion by telling him of the decision of the House of Lords. Tindal could hardly believe it possible. I agree with the *Times* that it would only be fair by O'Connell to allow him to stay in prison a few days longer, to consider what he is to do next." But O'Connell and the trial soon died away, and in the Session of 1846 the Maynooth grant was the subject which chiefly filled the minds of politicians. Mr. Gladstone resigned upon it, because he would not, while in office, support Sir Robert Peel's measure. Sir Robert endeavoured to strengthen his Cabinet by various changes, as to which Lord Palmerston makes the following suggestions as to his own office;—"If he would but shift Aberdeen to any other less important office, and put to the Foreign Office some man of more spirit, energy, and sagacity, it would be a great gain for the country; but that seems now hopeless!"

Then there came the step in English politics which Sir Robert Peel took in this Session, and by taking which he has obtained a place among the half-dozen greatest statesmen whom England has produced. He determined to repeal the Corn Laws altogether. "The Minister was honestly convinced," says Morley, in his "Life of Cobden," "but the party was not." How far the intention of his purpose came from the immediate necessity of his position,—how far, that is, we owed the repeal of the Corn Laws at that moment to the scarcity of food in Ireland,—or how far it was due to the actual conversion of the statesman's mind to the truth of Adam Smith's teaching, is, to my thinking, doubtful. There were yet five years before his death, and during those five years the conversion was completed. But the audacity with which he acted on the spur of the moment, resolving that a people must be fed even though he might have to abandon all his old political alliances, betokened a great man; and a great man he will remain as long as English history is read and understood. The political position at the moment, and that of Lord Palmerston as a person concerned, is so well described by Mr. Ashley that I will venture to quote his own words:—"The immediate cause of events, however, which came so suddenly on the political world, was a scarcity of the Irish potato crop. The population of Ireland had to be provided for;

and, after two or three meetings with his Cabinet, and propositions made by him and rejected by Lord Stanley, the Prime Minister declared that he saw no satisfactory course to adopt short of the total abolition of the Corn Laws, which it had been hitherto only proposed to modify; and the Administration broke up, Lord John Russell being entrusted with the construction of a new Ministry. This task, after a short effort to fulfil it, he resigned, giving as his principal reason for not forming a Government the refusal of Lord Grey to join it." This Lord Grey was the son of him who had refused to come back to the Government after Lord Althorp had become a peer. "If, as it was generally said, Lord Grey's refusal was because the Foreign Office was to be placed in the hands of Lord Palmerston, this would prove that all his former colleagues were not his friends, but that he still remained more powerful than his opponents. At all events, Sir Robert, exalted by the thought that he had a high duty to perform, once more sacrificed his past life to what he believed the future of his country, or perhaps (to speak more correctly) to the exigencies of the hour; and it was this disinterested conversion of an old and experienced statesman that gave the Manchester doctrines the unquestioned authority they have exercised from that time."

When the deed was done, the resignation of Sir Robert Peel was its only possible conclusion. Lord Stanley had already left the Ministry on the Corn Law question, and on the next important division which took place the Government was defeated by a union of the Whigs and Tories in the House of Commons. Sir Robert Peel retired, never again to return to office. Lord Palmerston sang the late Minister's pæan in the House of Commons, and then once more returned to the Foreign Office under the leadership of Lord John Russell.

❑❑❑

CHAPTER VII

Palmerston Foreign Secretary, July, 1846, To December, 1850

WE now come to Lord Palmerston's third period at the Foreign Office, which lasted from July, 1846, to December, 1851, but which we shall find it better to divide into three chapters than to comprise it in one, because it includes the romantic affair of Don Pacifico, which, by the attempts made and the success achieved, will deserve a chapter to itself. The *coup d'état* and his dismissal will demand a third. We will therefore take Lord Palmerston's life at the Foreign Office down to the year 1850, when the great Don Pacifico debate took place. There were in the meantime various circumstances, all at the moment of intense national interest, with which he was either specially concerned as Foreign Secretary, or much concerned as a leading Cabinet Minister. The chief among these were the Spanish marriages, Lord Minto's mission to Italy, the French Revolution and escape to England of Louis Philippe, the first war between Austria and Sardinia, the French occupation of Rome, and the wars in Hungary. With the minor operations of his official life it is impossible for us here to deal.

When he got back to office, there had arisen a question as to the expulsion of the Jesuits from certain Swiss cantons; but I do not know that the English reader will care much now about the Jesuits in Switzerland. Nor are we specially anxious as to the civil war which was then carried on in Portugal. But the knot in European politics known as the Spanish marriages had then an importance, and has since achieved results, which make it necessary that we should not altogether pass it over in any record, however short, of Lord Palmerston's life. But for those Spanish marriages Louis Philippe's heirs might still have sat upon the throne of France, and the name of king would not be altogether disgraced in the realm over which Henry IV. had ruled. No prophecy shall be ventured upon here as to the future of the French nation; but it is, I think, notorious to the world at large that the last blow given to the Bourbon family, in the opinion of Frenchmen, came from the Spanish marriages.

I cannot but here remark that, strong, abiding, and consistent as was Lord Palmerston's conduct in reference to these transactions, and assuredly as the disgrace would have been prevented could it have been staved off by our English Minister, he does not seem to speak of the foul political arrangements which were contemplated and carried out, with that disgust which they must have engendered in the mind of every honest and high-minded gentleman. But here we must remember that Lord Palmerston, as English Foreign Secretary, accustomed as he was to speak his mind freely, could not speak out quite plainly; and that of all that he did say we probably do not possess the whole. But the consequence is that up to this date men speak of the Spanish marriages as having been tolerable in politics though bad in morals, and as projects which should consign the inventors to no perdition, because they dealt, not with private, but with public matters. To us it has seemed that the evil intended, and in a great degree consummated, was of such a nature as to deserve all the stigma which a private iniquity could bear. The Spanish marriages are withdrawn from the comparatively easy regions of national conscience by the intensity of private desire for aggrandisement, by the private nature of the precautions taken, and by the private evil accomplished.

Now, I must tell the story with as little matter of annoyance as may be possible. It has already been told in Lord Palmerston's life, and so often before and since, that there can be no other reason for silence but the abomination of the tale to be told. It is, however, impossible to produce aright a memoir of Lord Palmerston's life without telling it. When kings and their councillors do amiss it is by no means the least of the evil done that their doings must be made public and explained.

It had become to be important to us and other nations that the thrones of France and Spain should be kept distinct, so that no French prince might come to sit upon the throne of Spain. As there were now two Spanish princesses,—Isabella, who was the Queen, and her sister, who at the moment was her heir,—Louis Philippe was required to engage, and did distinctly bind himself, that no son of his should marry Isabella, and also that no son of his should marry the sister till the Queen should have become a mother. Having bound himself by this undertaking the King's first endeavour was, to use an English phrase, to drive a coach and horses through it. He determined that a son of his, or at any rate a grandchild, should sit upon the throne of Spain, and presuming, as we must surmise, that he found his opportunity in the comparative weakness of Lord Aberdeen, he set to work to make such arrangements as might be practicable. Palmerston had declared in 1836, when Isabella was about five years old, that it would be so. "The fact is that he,"—Louis Philippe,—"is as ambitious as Louis XIV., and wants to put one of his sons on the throne of Spain as husband to the young Queen." But since then the young lady had grown to what in Spain is a marriageable age, and the young Prince who was to become the link between the thrones was twenty-two.

The King of the French did not see his way to break the engagement by running counter to its first clause. He could not marry his son to the young Queen. He might marry his son to the Queen's sister, as soon as that sister had a child. But that clause he did manage to break; and on the day on which the Queen was married, the Duke de Montpensier was married to the Princess. This was wrong, and false, and mischievous,—likely to lead to quarrels and wars, and unlikely to lead to increased power and dominion for any king or prince. But it was a trick within the compass of certain kings and certain ministers, and was not unroyal in all its bearings. Louis Philippe, however, was not contented with this. He went farther, and selected the Prince who was to marry the Queen. There was a Prince, unfortunate, as the minds of men go, but hitherto not disgraced,—a poor man who could never become the father of children. He it was whom Louis Philippe selected, with the assistance and guidance of Guizot, in the absolute ignorance, I do not hesitate to say, of Lord Aberdeen.

Such were the Spanish marriages. The fruits of them, as might have been guessed, were disastrous. The Queen, at any rate, had children, on whose royal birth no slur was openly thrown. The Duke de Montpensier lives as an unknown nobleman in a foreign land, to whose name there clings something of the flavour of his father's deeds. M. Guizot, who was the great Minister of the day, a man of high intellect, of thoughtful habits, of religious feeling, and a Protestant, tarnished his name for ever. And Louis Philippe ran from France as an exile, taking refuge in England under the name of Mr. Smith. And here he died! The marriages were perpetrated! But with what results to all who were concerned in them! It may be doubted whether any meaner crime was ever committed in the name of policy, or one of which the end was more befitting, or better deserved.

The effect which this produced in Europe took eighteen months to show itself. The marriages were solemnized in the autumn of 1846, and Louis Philippe came to England and took up his abode at Claremont in the spring of 1848. All his fine machinations had been blown like soap-bubbles into air! The result of the marriages upon English feeling, and upon Lord Palmerston, who was the one Englishman more concerned than others, was that of distinct alienation. It afforded matter but for few speeches in the House of Commons, and not much for private correspondence, as it was done in secret, and the wickedness of the arrangements could only creep out by slow degrees. Men at the time used to whisper to each other that it was so, and men who received the whisper declined to believe the story in all its foul enormity. Now it has become a matter of history, and there is no ordinary reader who does not know of what nature were the Spanish marriages. But Guizot is said at the time to have become so lost to all decent feeling, so warped and stung by the constant interference which he had received from

Lord Palmerston, as to have boasted that the political arrangement made was the one great thing which France had herself achieved, unaided, since 1830!

It effected the entire break-up of the concert which had existed between the great Powers of Europe, and clearly led to all the revolutions and disturbances of 1848. England and France were severed, and by their division Austria, Prussia and Russia were encouraged to expect to have their way. A further appropriation of Poland was intended, and was effected; but we find Palmerston endeavouring to prevent it. He writes to Lord Normanby on the 19th of November, 1846; "I have prepared an answer about Cracow, which I shall send off to Vienna without waiting for Guizot." "Guizot will make a show of resistance; but the fact is, that, even if France and England had been on good terms, they have no means of action on the spot in question, and could only have prevented the thing by a threat of war, which, however, the three Powers would have known we should never utter for the sake of Cracow. The measure is an abominable shame, and executed by the most hollow pretences and the most groundless assertions."

In January, 1847, the Queen protested, in her speech from the throne, against this new Polish outrage. Lord Palmerston was evidently nettled to think that he could not interfere so as to prevent it. It was but another scar on the Treaty of Vienna, and he could do nothing. Soon afterwards a French political officer of high standing had been condemned for corruption, and had endeavoured, or pretended to endeavour, to commit suicide. "In either way, these things must be a blow to Guizot and the Philippine system." The Philippine system was to Palmerston unutterably damnable. It was sly, fraudulent, false, extremely courteous, and thoroughly un-English. But it was secret, clever, and at this moment seemed to be triumphant. It was above all things opposed to Palmerston. We can conceive nothing more bitter than the hatred which at this time raged between the two statesmen. And in speaking of it, we should by no means endeavour to wash Lord Palmerston quite white. It may have been that had the "suaviter in modo" been more customary with him, the "fortiter in re" might have been more apparent. Being an older politician, and, we may say, a much wiser one, he had thought to dominate the Frenchman; but the Frenchman knew himself to possess a brighter intellect, a more brilliant style of eloquence, and, in erudition, to be the greater man. We will concede it to him,—that he was so. But Lord Palmerston possessed two virtues by means of which his name will go down to posterity altogether unsullied. He was brave, and he was honest.

We now come to Lord Minto's mission to Italy, which had been, we presume, arranged between Lord Palmerston and Lord John Russell. Pio Nono, the late Pope, had been elected in 1846, and Lord Minto started for Italy in November, 1846. We still remember how decided was the Liberalism of the new Pope, when he first filled St. Peter's chair,—an almost impossible condition for a Pope, and one which he soon vacated. But Lord Minto went to assist him in his Liberalism, to give him such aid as might be possible for an English Liberal Lord, and to find out in return what the new pope could do for England in keeping quiet seditious Irish bishops. "You will be at Rome," said Lord Palmerston, "not as a minister accredited to the Pope, but as an authentic organ of the British Government, enabled to explain its views and to declare its sentiments upon events which are now passing in Italy." "Her Majesty's Government are deeply impressed with the conviction that it is wise for Sovereigns and their Governments to pursue, in the administration of their affairs, a system of progressive improvement; to apply remedies to such evils as, upon examination, they may find to exist, and to re-model, from time to time, the ancient institutions of their country,—so as to render them more suitable to the gradual growth of intelligence, and to the increasing diffusion of political knowledge; and Her Majesty's Government consider it to be an undeniable truth, that if an independent Sovereign, in the exercise of his deliberate judgment, shall think fit to make within his dominions such improvements in the laws and institutions of his country as he may think conducive to the welfare of his people, no other Government can have any right to attempt to restrain or to interfere with such an employment of one of the inherent attributes of independent sovereignty."

We cannot but observe here the way in which Lord Palmerston lays down the law for the governance of the nations generally. No doubt he was right in what he said; but he said it with the air of some superior being, whose word is to go for more than the words of other mortals. Lord Minto does not go at once to Rome, but stays awhile at Turin, where the Austrians have shown a desire to interfere with Charles Albert, the father of Victor Emanuel. It is to be hoped that the Ambassador Extraordinary knew the phraseology of the hunting-field as well as did his correspondent. If so, he would understand when he was told that, "As to the Austrians they have been headed, and will not break cover towards Italy." Then Palmerston explains that, for having stopped the Austrians, the Pope ought to do him a good turn, in silencing a meddlesome bishop or two. Alas, that an opinion so absurd should ever have been held in regard to Pio Nono! "We wish to make the Pope the plain, and simple, and reasonable request that he will exert his authority over the Irish priesthood, to induce them to abstain from meddling in politics, but, on the contrary, to confine themselves to their spiritual duties." "I shall be able to send you by the next messenger, a memorandum about the letter which has recently been received by McHale, from Rome, upon the subject of the Irish colleges. This is an unkind and most mischievous measure, and was little to be expected at the hands of the Pope at the very moment we were stepping out of our way to be of use to him. It is an ungrateful return." And a little further on he writes to his correspondent; "You may confidently assure the Papal authorities that at present in Ireland, misconduct is the rule, and good conduct the exception, in the Catholic priests."

Of course it would be so, human nature being the same with Roman Catholics as with Protestants. Had we paid the priests, as we paid, and still pay, the parsons, out of the funds collected by the Government, the priests would have worked for the Government. To expect that they should do so under other circumstances is to dream of a Utopia. But to imagine that assistance could be got from the Pope to induce the priests to do so, was beyond any Utopian dream. There was a notion afloat at the time that the Pope should send an ambassador to London to carry out the liberal views with which he was supposed to have been imbued. But to this Lord Palmerston will give no assent. "As for the idea that we could manage the Irish priests by means of a Roman priest in London, I am convinced that the presence of such a man would only have given the Irish priests an additional means of managing us." Lord Minto writes back word that "The Pope is a most amiable, agreeable, and honest man, and sincerely pious to boot, which is much for a Pope; but he is not made to drive the State coach."

The honesty and piety of Pio Nono must be judged from his whole career. Certainly Lord Minto could not teach him the political state of Europe. "As to the poor Pope," says Lord Palmerston, writing back to Lord Minto, "I live in daily dread of some misadventure having befallen him. Events have gone too fast for such a slow sailer as he is." Then he speaks of the deposition of Guizot's ministry in Paris—for Guizot had been deposed. "What has been happening in Italy ought to have been a warning to Guizot. What has now happened to Guizot ought to be a warning to Italy. Guizot thought that by a packed Parliament and a corruptly-obtained majority, he could control the will of the nation, and the result has been that the will of the Crown has been controlled by an armed popular force. People have long gone on crying up Louis Philippe as the wisest of men. I always have thought him one of the most cunning, and therefore not one of the wisest. Recent events have shown that he must rank among the cunning, who outwit themselves; and not among the wise, who master events by foresight and prudence. This surrender of the King of the Barricades to the commons of the National Guard is, however, a curious example of political and poetical justice." This was in 1848, when all Europe was on the stir. "Was there ever such a scene of confusion as now prevails almost all over Europe? Fortunate, however, has it been for Italy that you crossed the Alps last autumn. If the Italian sovereigns had not been urged by you to move on, while their impatient subjects were kept back, there would by this time have been nothing but Republics from the Alps to Sicily." Then he ventures on a prophecy which has become absolutely true in later years. "We have just heard of the entrance of Sardinian troops into Lombardy to help the Milanese. Northern Italy will henceforth be Italian, and the Austrian frontier will be at the Tyrol. This will be no real loss to Austria." His dislike to Austria and Metternich is only second to his hatred for Louis Philippe and Guizot. France itself he did not hate, or even dislike—or, rather, liked as well as he could any country except England. He says that Austria after such losses may, if well governed, become a powerful State. But he adds: "The question is, Has she any men capable of making any State a powerful one by good government."

There had in the meantime sprung up a revolution in Sicily against Naples, and Lord Minto had gone on to Naples, and into the Sicilian waters, attempting to put it down. But it was not put down till 1849, when the seditious efforts of the previous year were nearly quelled throughout Europe. So Lord Minto returned home, having not apparently done much, but having brought with him more correct views of the Italian people than English Ministers had hitherto possessed.

Early in 1848 there came upon France that thorough disturbance of all things which has never yet quite rectified itself. Indeed, it may be said that there has been nearly a century of disturbance, during which, however, France has grown wonderfully in wealth and intelligence. But in 1830 France had once more re-established herself, and the Citizen King was put upon his throne as a thing of permanence and a just mixture of monarchical principles with democratic ideas. It must be acknowledged of Louis Philippe, as also of Napoleon III., that France did grow rich under him. But in both cases the riches came "post hoc" and not "propter hoc." According to our thinking, neither the one ruler nor the other could have benefited his people much, because neither of them was simple in his way of ruling. Louis Napoleon was yet to come, but Louis Philippe had now brought himself and his administration to an end.

There had been a great demand for reforms in Paris and the King had expressed himself strongly. "I never will consent to reform," he had exclaimed. "Reform is another word for the advent of the Opposition." "Tell your master not to mind having popular assemblies," is quoted by Lord Normanby as said by Louis Philippe to some foreign ambassador. "Let them only learn to manage things as I manage mine." The dismissal of Guizot, the Minister, was demanded among other things. Guizot had stood high for personal integrity;—and we believe that he was perfectly honest; but he got into various troubles in which he consented to the expenditure of public money to satisfy the rapacity of others; and, though he was honest himself, he seems to have dealt easily with dishonesty in his subordinates. But Louis Philippe felt that to lose Guizot was to own himself beaten, and clung to his Minister. Then came the proposition for a popular banquet, and the stopping of the banquet by the police, but with permission given for a procession; and then the stopping of the procession; and then the catastrophe. Louis Philippe, with his family, ran away, and in a few days appeared as Mr. Smith on the coast of Sussex, at Newhaven.

On the 26th of February Lord Palmerston thus writes to Lord Normanby; "What extraordinary and marvellous events you give me an account of. It is like the five acts of a play, and has not taken up much more time. Strange that a king who owed his crown to a revolution, brought about by royal blindness and obstinacy, should have lost it by exactly the same means, and he a man who had gone through all the vicissitudes of human existence, from the condition of a schoolmaster to the pomp of a throne; and still further that his overthrow should have been assisted by a Minister deeply read in the records of history, and whose mind was not merely stored with the chronology of historical facts, but had extracted from their mass the lessons of events and the philosophy of their causes." And then he gives instructions as to what shall be done by the English Ambassador in Paris. "Our principles of action are to acknowledge whatever rule may be established with apparent prospect of permanency, but none other." "We will engage to prevent the rest of Europe from meddling with France, which, indeed, we are quite sure they have no intention of doing. The French rulers must engage to prevent France from assailing any part of the rest of Europe." Then he goes on to lay down rules for different emergencies. What shall be done if the Revolution endeavours to protect itself by using the army for foreign conquest? But his heart beats warmly for his own child. "We cannot sit quiet and see Belgium overrun and Antwerp become a French port." "If they will look to the stipulations of the treaty finally concluded between the five Powers, Belgium, and the Netherlands, they will see that there are in it guarantees which would have a very awkward bearing upon any attempt by France to annex Belgium to its territory." He expresses his own feelings on the whole matter; "I grieve at the prospect of a Republic in France, for I fear it must lead to war in Europe and fresh agitation in England. Large Republics seem to be essentially and inherently aggressive, and the aggressions of the French will be resisted by the rest of Europe, and that is war; while, on the other hand, the example of universal suffrage in France will set our non-voting population agog, and will create a demand for an inconvenient extension of the franchise, ballot, and other mischievous things. However, for the present, 'Vive Lamartine!'" Lamartine was the provisional President of the New Republic, and while he remained in office did behave with a better grace than could have been expected from a man so abnormally situated.

"Here is a pretty to do at Paris," he says a few days later on in a letter to Lord Ponsonby at Vienna. "It is plain that, for the present at least, we shall have a Republic in France. How long it may last is another question. But for the present the only chance for tranquillity and order in France, and for peace in Europe, is to give support to Lamartine. I am convinced this French Government will not be aggressive if left alone. But if the Austrian Government does not mitigate its system of coercion in Lombardy and grant liberal institutions, they will have a revolt there." Our British difficulty at the moment arose chiefly from the advantage endeavoured to be taken by the Irish of the French revolutionary spirit. When all Europe was in revolt Ireland, of course, would not remain calm. Smith O'Brien with various deputations was at once in Paris. "I have written to you," says Lord Palmerston to Lord Normanby, "an official despatch about M. De Lamartine's allocutions to Irish despatches and his direct allusions therein to our internal affairs, such as Catholic Emancipation, Irish agitation, Repeal of the

Union, and other matters, with which no foreign Government had any right to meddle. I wish you to convey to him, in terms as civil as you can use, that these speeches, and especially that to which my despatch refers, have given great offence in this country." It does not appear to have occurred to him how often he himself was interfering in the foreign affairs of other countries. But Lamartine seems to have taken the observations in good part. "Pray tell Lamartine," he says, "how very much obliged we feel for his handsome and friendly conduct about the Irish deputations."

The amount of business which fell on to his shoulders at this time may be well imagined, and yet he was now sixty-four years old. "As to your not always getting letters from me by every messenger who passes through Paris, never wonder at that, nor think it extraordinary." This is still to Lord Normanby. "Wonder rather when I am able to find time at all. I am sure you would if you saw the avalanches of despatches from every part of the world which come down upon me daily, and which must be read, and if you witnessed the number of interviews which I cannot avoid giving every day of the week. Every post sends me a lamenting minister throwing himself and his country upon England for help, which I am obliged to tell him we cannot afford him. But Belgium is a case by itself, and both France and England are bound by treaty engagements in regard to that country, which it is most desirable for the repose of France and England that no events should call into active operation." Then he sends word to our Ambassador at St. Petersburg as to what may there be expected of England in reference to certain Polish difficulties which have cropped up. "We, the Government, will never do anything underhand or ungentlemanlike in these matters. I wish we could hope that the Emperor might of his own accord settle the Polish question in some satisfactory manner." Then there is an allusion to the one burlesque English incident which graced the Revolution. "I conclude that he"—he is Lamartine—"has escaped one danger by the refusal to naturalize Brougham; for it is evident that our ex-Chancellor meant, if he got himself elected, to have put up for being President of the Republic."

In 1848, as a part of the European disturbance, the Chartist rows came up in London, affording the most signal evidence that up to that time at least the spirit of democratic enmity to order was not at work in England. Nor, according to such evidence as we possess, is it so now,—though at this moment, 1882, it is rampant in Ireland. The question was one with which Lord Palmerston had not much immediate concern. But, alluding to his branch of politics, he writes with his usual vivacity. "The foreigners did not show; but the constables, regular and special, had sworn to make an example of any whiskered and bearded rioters whom they might meet with, and I am convinced would have mashed them to a jelly."

Then he interested himself very strongly in the attempt which was made in 1848 to banish the Austrians from the North of Italy. "Things have gone much too far to admit of the possibility of any future connection between the Italians and Austria." And again, "I certainly agree with you and your Austrian friend that Austria would be much better out of Italy than in it. Italy can never now be a useful possession for Austria." And again, "On the whole, the conclusion to which I should come is, that the cheapest, best, and wisest thing which Austria can do, is to give up her Italian possessions quietly and at once, and to direct her attention and energy to organizing the remainder of her coast territories, and to cement them together, and to develop their abundant resources;"—to induce the Austrians to abandon their Austrian possessions as a matter of pure policy. "But to do this there ought to be some able men at the head of affairs, and our doubt is whether there are any such now in office. First and foremost, what is the animal *implumis bipes*, called Emperor? A perfect nullity; next thing to an idiot." Then he discusses the practicability of an abdication, or rather two abdications, with a wisdom and foresight to which events have given their ample testimony. Francis Joseph, the Emperor of to-day, was, after a while, elected in place of his uncle, and has since reigned, through many troubles, with good sense and moderation.

"How can an empire stand in these days without an emperor at its head? And by an emperor, I mean a man endowed with intellectual faculties suited to his high station." And again, "I fear that his next brother is little better than he is; but could not the son of that brother be called to the succession?" But it is remarkable that this is all written to our ambassador at Vienna, and is written as advice to be given to an Austrian Minister. "Pray then, tell Wessemberg from me, but in the strictest confidence, that I would entreat of him and his colleagues to consider, for the salvation of their country, whether some arrangement could not be made by which the Emperor might abdicate." Can we imagine any foreign minister recommending to an English statesman the abdication of a British sovereign? In this case, no doubt, the abdication had been previously discussed; but still the audacity, necessary for such advice from an Englishman, was very great. Fighting, however, in the meantime, was going on, and Radetsky, on the part of Austria, was victorious at Milan. France and England joined to assist Sardinia by their moral weight, and an armistice was concluded.

But Palmerston will not give up his points. "The real fact is that the Austrians have no business in Italy at all, and have no real right to be there." This he writes to Lord Ponsonby at Vienna, and says very evil things of the Austrian mode of governing. "The only Austrians have been the troops, and the civil officers. She has governed it as you govern a garrison town, and her rule has always been hateful." Then he expresses his strong resentment against attempts which have been made from Vienna, or which he thinks have been made, to influence the English Court. "I quite understand the drift and meaning of Prince Windischgrätz's message to our Queen; but pray make the Camarilla understand that, in a constitutional country like England, these things cannot answer; and that a foreign Government, which places its reliance upon working upon the Court against the Government of this country, is sure to be disappointed." But in his strong feeling against Austria and in favour of Italy, in his passionate dislike to the Austrian mode of government, and his strong love for that which he believed would be the Italian mode of government in Italy, he runs into some absurdities which are contradicted in the same letter. "Providence," he says, "meant mankind to be divided into separate nations, and for this purpose countries have been founded by natural barriers, and races of men have been distinguished by separate languages, habits, manners, dispositions, and characters." Then he goes on; "North of the Alps, we wish her"—that is Austria—"all the prosperity and success in the world;" though the Austrian and the Hungarian are also distinguished by separate language, habits, and manners. But for the moment the contest was brought to an end by the victory of Austria, and ten years had to pass by before Lord Palmerston saw all his hopes for Italy realized by the unification of the country under the Sardinian crown.

Before the close of the Session in 1849 Mr. Disraeli brought on a vote of want of confidence in the Government. Lord Palmerston writes thus to his brother; "After all the trumpetings of attacks that were to demolish first one and then another member of the Government—first me, then Grey, then Charles Wood—we have come triumphantly out of all debates and divisions, and end the Session, stronger than we began it. Our division this morning, on Disraeli's motion 'On the State of the Nation,' was 296 to 156—a majority of 140." And in the House of Lords, Lord Brougham fared no better. "Sicily, Lombardy and Rome will be the main topics on which Brougham, Stanley and Aberdeen—the three witches who have filled the cauldron—will dilate." France had at this time "occupied" Rome. "The questions which will naturally be asked are; In what character has the French army taken possession of Rome? Is it as conquerors of a city to be added to France? Of course not; that answer is easily given. Is it, then, as friends of the Pope, or as friends of the Roman people?" It was a question which would naturally be asked. But the French had taken possession of Rome to guard it equally from the Pope and from the people. The above was written on the 16th July, 1849. On the previous 24th of November the Pope had escaped from Rome in disguise, and had got as far as Gaeta on his way to Majorca. He did not go further on that journey, and there we may leave him, remarking that it was less than thirty months since he had received as a reforming Pope professions of universal affection from the Roman people.

Lord Palmerston feels himself compelled to ask hypothetical questions of the French Government, and to put hypothetical answers into its mouth. We can see that he is in truth jealous that there is a European pie in which he is not allowed to have a finger. But there is not a word in what he says in which an ordinary Englishman does not sympathize. "There are mutually repellent properties between a reasoning people and an elective priestly Government." "The Roman people will ere long reply by saying; We are no longer Papists; take your Pope and give him as sovereign to those who are Papists still. The Reformation in Europe was as much a movement to shake off political oppression as it was to give freedom to religious conscience, and similar causes are apt to produce similar effects." Then there has come an attack upon him as Foreign Minister from Lord Aberdeen, whom he takes an opportunity of "paying off," as he calls it. He does pay him off—with great severity, with good thorough-going abuse, which is, however, altogether parliamentary. The entire speech is too long to be given here with the necessary explanations. But he winds up as follows; "I will only say that the conduct of such men is an example of antiquated imbecility." The "such men" is, of course, Lord Aberdeen. The next day, no doubt, he would have been on excellent terms with Lord Aberdeen had he met him.

Then, still in 1849, there is a difficulty as to the amount of assistance to be given to Turkey in holding her own against Austria and Russia. The Hungarian conflict had come on, in which Hungary had endeavoured to maintain her own kingdom and her own government, as separated from that of Austria. The Hungarians were willing that the Emperor of Austria should be King of Hungary, but refused to assent to any other joining of the two countries. Here again Palmerston had not his fingers very deep in the pie. How far he may have been restrained by colleagues in his Cabinet, we do not know; but we do remember how, when Austria was hard pressed by her rebels, she was assisted by Russia; and we do know, also, how ungratefully Austria behaved on the occasion. But when the Hungarians were beaten, some of their leaders, and Kossuth among them, escaped into Turkey. Then

Russia and Austria demanded the extradition of these rebels, and the Sultan was encouraged to withhold them by Sir Stratford Canning, who now first comes forward as the great friend of the Porte.

Lord Palmerston also warmly takes the part of the Turks, and will not allow the men to be surrendered. It is this affair which gives the chief interest to the autumn of 1849. He writes on the matter very hotly to Lord Ponsonby. "As to working upon their feelings of generosity and gentlemanlikeness"—the feelings of the Austrians—"that is out of the question, because such feelings exist not in a set of officials who have been trained up in the school of Metternich, and the men in whose minds such inborn feelings have not been crushed by Court and office power, have been studiously excluded from public affairs, and can only blush in private for the disgrace which such things throw upon their country. But I do hope that you will not fail constantly to bear in mind the country and the Government which you represent, and that you will maintain the dignity and honour of England by expressing openly and decidedly the disgust which such proceedings excite in the public mind in this country." It is evident that he had heard something of which he does not approve in Lord Ponsonby's mode of thinking. "The remedy against these various dangers, which are rapidly undermining the Austrian Empire, would be generous conciliation; but instead of that, the Austrian Government knows no method of administration but what consists in flogging, imprisoning, and shooting. The Austrians know no argument but force." The two fleets (the English and the French) were moved up to the Dardanelles. "In this affair we are trying to catch two great fish, and we must wind the reel very gently and dexterously, not to break the line." This he says to Sir Stratford Canning. He declares to Brunnow, "That our sending our squadron up the Mediterranean was, for the Sultan, like holding a bottle of salts to the nose of a lady who had been frightened." Of course he has his way, and Turkey is not allowed to give up the Hungarians, though he ascertains in the course of the correspondence that Lord Ponsonby, his own ambassador at Vienna, is opposed to the instructions which he receives. But he reprimands him at last with severity. "I write you this, and desire you to do your best; though I hear from many quarters that you oppose instead of furthering the policy of your Government, and that you openly declare that you disapprove of our course. No diplomatist ought to hold such language as long as he holds his appointment."

CHAPTER VIII

The Story of Don Pacifico

THE story of Don Pacifico is interesting, dramatic, and peculiar, and emblematic in the highest degree of Lord Palmerston's manner of feeling and condition of mind. In it he will be seen carrying British honesty, British honour, and British determination to the very verge of absurdity and arrogance, till he pushes his principles almost beyond the verge. But who shall say what is absurdity? And he is held to have been thoroughly triumphant in the whole affair, because at last he got a majority of the House of Commons to vote that he had been splendidly English and splendidly honest rather than absurd and arrogant. We may be sure that the statesmen of other nations ridiculed him, but that they did so with a mixture of awe, knowing that it was Palmerston,—and knowing that Palmerston must be allowed to have his own way in such matters,—unless he were stopped by his own countrymen. And a great attempt was made by his own countrymen to keep him down, and to prove that he had been ridiculous. Lord Stanley, who, since 1844, had been in the Upper House, brought a direct motion against him, in which he was supported by Lord Aberdeen and Lord Canning; and he carried his resolution by a majority of thirty-seven. Lord Stanley had not forgotten the accusations of official ignorance made against him by Lord Palmerston; and Lord Aberdeen's memory was still laden with the bitterness of that "example of antiquated imbecility," as which he had been represented to the House of Commons. For amenities such as these Lord Palmerston was too wise to expect in return aught but similar amenities.

"I can only say," said Lord Stanley, "that I have arisen from the perusal of these papers,"—and he describes the documents in his hands, all referring to claims made by Lord Palmerston against Greece, as a weary waste of papers,—"with regret and shame for the part which my country has played." Then he takes the proud ground that the weakest and the strongest nations should in such matters be treated alike; and he asks whether such has been the case—imputing, of course, to Lord Palmerston the degrading fault that he has been imperious only against the weak. Then he recapitulates the absurd cases for redress as to which Lord Palmerston sent the British Fleet to the Piræus,—a fleet larger, as Lord Aberdeen goes on to say, than that with which Nelson conquered at Trafalgar. Can this, we wonder, have been true? There is the matter of Stellio Sumachi, the blacksmith, which was of itself a very trivial affair. Then there was the question of two of our war vessels, the *Fantôme* and the *Spitfire*. A midshipman out of one had landed in plain clothes where he ought not to have landed, and officers of the one ship were taken to have been officers of the other. This had given ground for great offence to British honour. There was the plunder of some Ionian boats at Salcina, Ionians being regarded in Athens as being Greeks well able to take care of themselves,—whereas to Lord Palmerston they were British subjects. Then there was the case of certain Ionians who had laid themselves down in the street to get rid of the fleas which were intolerable in their houses. With these men the police had interfered, as they certainly should not have interfered with British subjects afraid of fleas. Then there was a bit of ground, which Mr. Finlay had bought for £10 or £20, amounting to less than an acre. This was included in King Otho's garden without payment, whereas a Britisher should, of course, have been paid,—and Mr. Finlay demanded about £1,500. He did ultimately get £1,000. And lastly there was Don Pacifico, the Jew. It had been the custom of the Greeks at a certain festival to burn the figure of Judas; but one of the Rothschilds had come to Athens, and it was thought that this Christian ceremony would be distasteful to him. Therefore the Greeks omitted to burn the Judas, but did burn Don Pacifico's house, and among the rioters who burnt it was the son of the Greek Minister of War. Now, Don Pacifico, though his relations were supposed to have been Portuguese-Jews, had resided at Gibraltar, or, as some said, had been born there. He had at any rate made out for himself some claim to British citizenship. It sufficed for Lord Palmerston; but the amount of compensation claimed by Don Pacifico was, among the many absurdities, the most absurd. There were certain Portuguese documents which were represented as of immense value. They had been burned, and £26,000 had been charged for them, though they seem to have consisted only of letters from Don Pacifico in which he made his claim, and from the Portuguese Government denying that anything was due to him. All these points Lord Stanley exposed, and he ended by moving; "That, while the House fully recognizes the right and duty of the Government to secure to her Majesty's subjects residing in Foreign States the full protection of the laws of those States, it regrets to find, by the correspondence recently laid upon the table by her Majesty's command, that various claims against the Greek Government, doubtful in points of justice, or exaggerated in amount, have been enforced by coercive measures, directed against the commerce and people of Greece, and calculated to endanger the continuance of our friendly relations with other Powers." He carried his motion, as I have said, by thirty-seven votes. During the debate, Lord Aberdeen spoke of the "cry of indignation" which had been called forth throughout Europe by the doings of our fleet; and Lord Cardigan threatened the peers with a great war.

The joy was great among Lord Palmerston's enemies; and it will be understood that they were numerous. He had against him generally the diplomacy of Europe. First of all the French were very hostile to him. The hostility of Thiers and Guizot still remained, kept warm among the archives of the French Foreign Office. And the Austrians and the Prussians and the Russians were all hostile to him;—and the Bavarians, of whose king, Otho, the young king of Greece, was son. The French, as he complains, were treating him with gross ingratitude. When the French were making demands on Morocco, which Palmerston himself describes as "unusual and exaggerated," had not our consul, "first spontaneously, and then by instructions from me," and "by an infinity of trouble," talked the Moors into paying? But, he tells Lord Normanby, that when we ask for our own, "we find the French Minister, faithful to the course which French diplomacy has for years past pursued in Greece, encouraging the Greek Government to refuse, and thus doing all he can to drive us to the necessity of employing force to obtain redress." And even among Englishmen a strong party has been made against him. Even his own friend Lord Normanby, his own ambassador in Paris, does not seem to have assisted him with his whole heart in what he was doing. "As to the melodrama which you talk of, it seems to me to have been the right course." "But we have all along been thwarted in Greece by the intrigues and cabals of French agents, who have encouraged the Greek Government to ill-use our subjects and to refuse us satisfaction, and of course Thouvenel is frantic that at last we have lost patience." And Russia is as hostile as France. He writes to Lord Bloomfield; "We do not mind the Russian swagger and attempt to bully about Greece. We shall pursue our own course steadily and firmly, and we must and shall obtain the satisfaction we require." "I have been so busy fighting my battle with France, that I have been obliged to put off for a time taking up again my skirmish with Russia." "There have been in London within the last week letters from Madame Lieven to friends of hers here, abusing me like a pickpocket." And he complains of our own newspapers. In writing to the Prime Minister, he talks of "the boastful threats made by the *Times* newspaper as to what Russia would do to put a stop to our proceedings in Greece." Then again he writes to Lord John as to a question which is to be brought before the Cabinet on the next day. He has already obtained a deposit from the Greek Government, and the question is mooted whether the deposit shall not be returned. "Normanby's conversation with the President brings another question under the consideration of the Cabinet. Louis Napoleon would be satisfied, as I infer, if to the arbitration we added the restitution of the deposit, and this the Cabinet will have to consider to-morrow. The reasons for and against seem to me to be much as follows." He then proceeds to explain why he thinks the deposit should be kept in hand, and he evidently feels that the Cabinet may be against him. Indeed, he fears that many are opposed to him who should be his friends, as well as all who are naturally his enemies. And we can see that it is not about this affair of Don Pacifico that his mind is anxious. Don Pacifico is such a flea as that which disturbed the slumbers of the British Ionians. And Greece, with its freedom, of which by this time Palmerston had become nearly sick, was not much more. Shall he, or shall he not, be able to hold his head on high amidst the deep Court waters, in which he had so long been struggling? For the battle with him was one against the absolutism of rulers, on behalf of the constitutional rule of nations. With the rulers were their favourites and Ministers,—and indeed masters; for who need be told that a Metternich was, in fact, master in the Court of Vienna? "We have long had all these things in our own hands," we can imagine they would say to themselves. "All the glory and the power, and the silks and the satins, and the soft words and courtly shows of imperial rule; and here is this man, who has crept in among us; and has become by his own audacity the first of our order, and is daily lecturing us as to the way in which we shall do our business! And at the bottom is he not as abominable a Revolutionist as any of them? Are we not, among us, able to put him down; and shall we not use the power which, by the excess of his own arrogance, he has now given us?" Thus it is we can imagine that they spoke among themselves, not without sundry endeavours to inveigle his own servants in their own Courts. And we can imagine also in what language Palmerston spoke to himself, when he looked round about him in the world and saw what was going on. He had been continually prompted to arrogance by the conviction that in no other way could he withstand the counts and barons, the duchesses and princesses. He must have known of himself that he was arrogant; but he must have known also that when he would yield an inch he would at once fall, an ell at a time. The motives in men's minds are mixed. We do believe that with him a true love of liberty had grown up amidst his Foreign Office duties, forcing him to think rather of the English nation than of the ways of Courts. But there had grown with it a lust of personal power and a desire to rule from his desk in Downing Street as much of Europe as he could get into his hands. So should the Turk do under certain circumstances, and so the Austrian, so the Russian, so the Greek, and the Spaniard,—and so, also, as far as might be possible, the Frenchman. Of course, with so many efforts, he often failed; but as he went on he saw, or thought he saw, that where he failed there had come misfortune to the world at large; and where he had succeeded, prosperity.

When he had found, or thought that he had found, that a thing was just, he would have his own way, and was not unfrequently earned astray from justice in the pursuit of power. Greece had become to him a very stumbling-block of offences. Prince Otho of Bavaria, who had been sent there to be King, hardly with Palmerston's assent, had not at all answered the purpose of his mission. The Constitutional Government which was promised had been delayed, and was never really established under King Otho. Misrule of all kinds became rampant; and matters arose which, with all his patience, must have driven Palmerston nearly mad in his efforts to keep men—not right, but from drifting into recognized illegality. That Mr. Finlay, who had bought his bit of ground, and had had it taken from him without payment and could get not even an answer when he sent in his bill, must have been a provoking stumbling-block. So also was Don Pacifico, with his abominable pettifogging Levant lies and his Jew villanies. I can imagine that, though it did not suit Lord Palmerston openly to abuse Don Pacifico, he must have hated him in the core of his heart. And those flea-bitten Ionians, and even the silly English sailors, must have been distasteful to him. Such a bill as Don Pacifico sent in! There were sofas, ottomans, and consoles of most portentous manufacture; and, above all things, there was a *lit conjugal*, which must have been surely kept for the expected arrival of a young Duke and Duchess. Lord Stanley says he prefers, in giving the inventory of the furniture, the language of Don Pacifico to the more homely phrase, a double-bed. And then those Portuguese documents,—invaluable, not to be replaced, and now gone for ever!

Lord Palmerston of course knew, as well as did Lord Stanley, that Don Pacifico's bill was a hideous Levant fraud from beginning to end, having its only base of justice in the fact that the Greek Government had refused to acknowledge it at all. A Greek, of some position in his country, had been present in the streets encouraging the rioters when the house had been burnt down, and the police had refused to notice the matter. Application over and over again had been made for redress,—that due inquiries should at any rate be made; but nothing had been done, and Lord Palmerston would not put up with it Don Pacifico was the last ounce which broke the camel's back. No doubt Greece was a difficulty to him, and specially a difficulty because she was powerless to protect herself. King Otho and his Ministers were probably instigated by others to use their own weakness. When Great Britain finds a difference between herself and France or the United States, no doubt she must bide her time and wait till just inquiries have been made before true justice shall have been,—or shall not have been, discovered. But with Greece,—with Greece who was there as a separate nation, partly, if not mainly, by his own efforts,—it was out of the question that Great Britain should allow herself to be laughed at. It was at any rate, out of the question with Lord Palmerston. So he sent a fleet,—perhaps larger than was necessary,—to exact damages. Certainly it was larger if it would have sufficed at the date of Trafalgar to beat the united navies of France and Spain;—but we doubt the fact. "Even this Pacifico,—this vile Portuguese Jew, this scum of the Mediterranean,—shall have such justice as he may deserve; and if he have much more than justice, that will be the fault of those who refused to inquire into the matter when some inquiry was possible." It was thus, that we can imagine Palmerston to have spoken to himself.

The matter took wide proportions and loomed large as though it would assume European greatness. Baron Gros was sent from France as a mediator, and the French Ambassador was actually withdrawn from London. It is hardly necessary now to make all the ins and outs intelligible to the reader. At last the matter was settled. Mr. Finlay was paid and Don Pacifico received compensation. Lord Palmerston had so far been victorious. But the time had come in which the contest was to be transferred from the Piræus, and to be fought out in London. It has been told how Lord Stanley, whom we remember better now as Lord Derby, and Lord Aberdeen, had risen in their wrath, backed by Lord Cardigan and the majority of the Peers generally. What influence had been at work who can say? But it was natural that such influence should prevail. That Lord Stanley did blush for his country, and that Lord Aberdeen did hear a cry of indignation, and Lord Cardigan fear a general war, was, perhaps, true. But the blushes and the cry and the fears were extended only to a limited area. The Princes and the Countesses blushed and feared. The Lords having carried their resolution showed no purpose of going any further. But Lord Palmerston having been so treated could not allow the matter to rest there. He was not a man specially fond of making speeches; but here was a case in which, unless a speech could be made to some effect, he must acknowledge himself to have been beaten. In the House of Lords Viscount Canning, the son of Lord Palmerston's old master in politics, and who afterwards served in the Cabinet with him and was his Governor-General for India, finished his speech as follows; "If it was fated that a page in their history must be defaced by the record of a policy founded on injustice, conducted with arrogance, and closed without dignity, let them at least have the consolation to know that the same page would bear witness that their policy received, at the earliest opportunity circumstances would permit, its direct, deliberate, and unqualified condemnation in a censure of the House of Lords." Lord Canning was not then so great a man as he became afterwards; but it was necessary that language such as this should receive a direct refutation in the House of Commons, seeing that it had been asserted in the House of Lords. If this could not have been made to come to pass Lord Palmerston must have retired.

On June 17, 1850, the debate took place in the House of Lords. As no hostile motion was intended to follow up in the House of Commons the hostility of the Lords, the matter must be met by a movement on the other side. There was a consultation, no doubt, between Palmerston and certain of his friends, and it was decided that the service of Mr. Roebuck should be employed,—more especially as Mr. Roebuck had more than once opposed the foreign policy of the great Foreign Minister. There was some flattery in the selection no doubt, but it availed. On June 24, therefore the member for Sheffield moved that "The principles on which the foreign policy of Her Majesty's Government have been regulated have been such as were calculated to maintain the honour and dignity of this country; and, in times of unexampled difficulty, to preserve peace between England and the various nations of the world." Mr. Roebuck, though his speech was long and somewhat inflated, did represent the matter well, looking at it from Lord Palmerston's side.

Then arose a debate as of the gods,—remarkable among debates for the length and strength of the speakers, as also, in the case of many of them, for the excellence of their speeches. Sir Frederick Thesiger was longer than Mr. Roebuck, and Sir James Graham almost as long. They were men conspicuous then among Tories, and they both did their best against the Foreign Secretary. That Lord John Manners should have done so, and Sidney Herbert, and Sir Robert Peel,—who now, alas, spoke for the last time in that House,—and Mr. Disraeli, the lion and the lamb thus lying down together, was what we should have expected to find on looking back to the debate. But Sir W. Molesworth spoke on the same side, and Mr. Cobden, both, no doubt, moved by high ideas of conscience. The strongest speech of all, however, as against the Government, and the most damning to Lord Palmerston, was that spoken by Mr. Gladstone, who, sitting on the Tory benches, rose in his rage, and laid about him with all that damaging passion of which he was then, when a Tory, almost as great a master as he has since proved himself in the Liberal ranks. As this is a short memoir of Lord Palmerston's life, I cannot deal at length with Mr. Gladstone's speech on that occasion. We can see him, however, and hear him as he rebukes the weary House. "What, sir, are there gentlemen in this House who can pursue their idle chat while words like these are sounding in their ears? If there are, I must tell them frankly that I am not a little mortified at their withholding from myself the compliment of their attention." And again, he is Gladstone himself, as he speaks of what the mighty owe to the feeble. "No, sir, let it not be so. Let us recognize, and recognize with frankness, the equality of the weak with the strong, the principles of brotherhood among nations and of their sacred independence." There were giants also on the Government side of the House. Bernal Osborne, Sir George Grey, Monckton Milnes, and Lord John Russell all spoke well. But among those who supported Lord Palmerston, Mr. Cockburn, our Lord Chief Justice afterwards, was the most effective. His speech to this day is admirable reading, as indeed were many of the speeches then made. Baillie Cochrane, now Lord Lamington, who had long been a popular member of the House, had written a pamphlet strongly condemnatory of Greece and of the gross injustice which prevailed there. But Mr. Cochrane was a Tory,—a very decided Tory,—and had spoken against Palmerston in this debate with violence, and he now heard the words he had printed read to him with great effect by Mr. Cockburn. A more telling speech on Mr. Roebuck's side could not have been made than this quotation, as showing the impossibility of obtaining redress by law in Greece.

But the one speech of the occasion was that delivered by Lord Palmerston, and it was the greatest speech he ever made. It proved that had he chosen to devote himself to that branch of politics, he could have become a great orator. The debate lasted for four nights, and this speech occupied four hours and a half. He was, in truth, pleading for his life. And yet he seemed to take it quite calmly, and did not, during the whole of the four hours, allow himself to be carried into any violence. He went on with his arguments, never allowing them to fall flatly, but seldom attempting to rise to any excessive height. He laid down his idea as to the redress to which an Englishman is entitled. "I say, then, that our doctrine is, that, in the first instance, redress should be sought from the law courts of the country; but that in cases where redress cannot be so had,—and those cases are many,—to confine a British subject to that remedy only would be to deprive him of the protection which he is entitled to receive."

Going on to the special case of Don Pacifico, he then explains the circumstances. "What happened in this case? In the middle of the town of Athens, in a house which I must be allowed to say is not a wretched hovel, as some people have described it,—but it does not matter what it is, for whether a man's home be a palace or a cabin, the owner has a right to be there safe from injury,—well, in a house which is not a wretched hovel, but which, in the early days of King Otho, was, I am told, the residence of the Count Armansperg, the chief of the Regency,—a house as good as the generality of those which existed in Athens before the sovereign ascended the throne,—M. Pacifico, living in that house, within forty yards of the great street, within a few minutes walk of a guard-house where soldiers were stationed, was attacked by a mob. Fearing injury when the mob began to assemble, he sent an intimation to the British Minister, who immediately informed the authorities. Application was made to the Greek Government for protection. No protection was afforded. The mob, in which were soldiers and gens-d'armes, who even, if officers were not with them, ought, from a sense of duty, to have interfered and to have prevented plunder,—that mob, headed by the sons of the Minister of War, not children of eight or ten years old, but older,—that mob for nearly two hours employed themselves in gutting the house of an unoffending man, carrying away or destroying every single thing the house contained, and left it a perfect wreck."

Then he passes on to the general foreign policy of his administration, and answers the charges which had been made against him at great length by Sir James Graham. We cannot follow him here, as to do so we should be driven to go back over the whole work of his life. But the clearness with which it is all done is of such a nature that no one can now obtain a more lucid statement of the English view of European politics during the period; and he then concludes his view of the manner in which Great Britain could wish that her foreign affairs should be governed, and in which he thinks that they have been governed by him. "I do not complain of the conduct of those who have made these matters the means of attack upon Her Majesty's Ministers. The Government of a great country like this is undoubtedly an object of fair and legitimate ambition to men of all shades of opinion. It is a noble thing to be allowed to guide the policy, and to influence the destinies of such a country; and, if ever it was an object of honourable ambition, more than ever must it be so at the moment at which I am speaking. For while we have seen, as stated by the right honourable baronet the member for Ripon, the political earthquake rocking Europe from side to side,—while we have seen thrones shaken, shattered, levelled,—institutions overthrown and destroyed,—while in almost every country of Europe the conflict of civil war has deluged the land with blood, from the Atlantic to the Black Sea, from the Baltic to the Mediterranean, this country has presented a spectacle honourable to the people of England, and worthy of the admiration of mankind."

The speech was liked by the whole House, foes as well as friends. It was thus that all Englishmen felt that they would wish that an English Minister of State should defend himself and the Government to which he belonged. "It has made us all proud of him," said poor Sir Robert Peel, who, after that day, never lived to express such pride again. Then came the division; and, in a House of five hundred and seventy-four members, Lord Palmerston was acquitted by a majority of forty-six. On the next day,—or, in truth, on that day, for the division was not taken till nearly four o'clock,—he sent a word of joy over to Lord Normanby. "Our triumph has been complete in the debate, as well as in the division; and, all things considered, I scarcely ever remember a debate which, as a display of intellect, oratory, and high and dignified feeling, was more honourable to the House of Commons."

There never had been a pitched battle fought on that arena in which the thing to be fought for was better understood, in which the combatants were marshalled in fairer order, in which the strategy was of a higher nature, or the courage displayed more brilliant. Should the Whigs, plus Palmerston, be kept in office, or should they be expelled from office because of Palmerston's ungovernable arrogance? The House of Commons and the Whigs determined to keep Palmerston in his place. The victory was very great, and the glory almost unbounded. The House of Lords was set at naught, and a majority of forty-six in the House of Commons was taken as showing the will of the entire nation.

But it was not to last for long. Lord Palmerston knew, or asserted that he knew, where lay the real force which he had to encounter; and though he sounded his trumpet loudly on the occasion, and in the moment of his triumph forgot that his enemies still existed, he lived to remember their power. He thus wrote to his brother William; "The attack on our foreign policy has been rightly understood by everybody as the shot fired by a foreign conspiracy, aided and abetted by domestic intrigue." He goes on in the same letter to tell how he was invited to dinner by two hundred and fifty members of the Reform Club, and how the banquet might have been extended to a thousand had it not been thought well to limit the demonstration. It was after this victory that the famous portrait of Lord Palmerston was painted, and presented to Lady Palmerston, by a hundred and twenty members of the House of Commons. This period,—the end, that is, of the session of 1850,—was the culminating point in the fortunes of our great Foreign Minister. He lived, indeed, to be twice Premier, and to have superintended the counsels by which Nicholas was beaten to his death in the Crimean War; but I do not think that he was ever as great as on the night on which he defended himself for having protected Don Pacifico. Such is the story of Don Pacifico. How the battle was renewed under other auspices in the next year, and how Lord Palmerston was then dismissed by the same Lord John Russell who now had defended him, must be told in the next chapter.

❑❑❑

CHAPTER IX

Palmerston as Foreign Secretary Till His Dismissal, in 1851

LORD PALMERSTON achieved his triumph in 1850, and encountered his disgrace, if it is to be so considered, in 1851. There was but the one year and a few months before his foes were too many for him. In describing this second battle, I shall endeavour to tell the story as though the blow had come from Lord John Russell, the head of the Cabinet, with such aid and counsel as may have been given to him by others of his own class. Of the action of the Court, as told to us in detail by Sir Theodore Martin, I have spoken in the first chapter, and it will be more convenient if I go on with Lord Palmerston's career without much further allusion to it. He himself believed that he had been the victim of a foreign conspiracy, aided by those Englishmen who agreed that its purpose was good. In September, 1850, he thus wrote to his brother,—after the affair of Don Pacifico; "I have beaten and put down and silenced, at least for a time, one of the most widespread and malignant and active confederacies that ever conspired against one man without crushing him; but I was in the right, and I was able to fight my battle." "The death of Louis Philippe delivers me from my most artful and inveterate enemy, whose position gave him in many ways the power to injure me." The readers of to-day will dislike the use of the word conspiracy, and will think that the powers brought to bear against the Foreign Secretary were no more than those of fair political opposition. And it will probably be thought that Lord Palmerston was becoming too powerful in foreign affairs,—or was wont to express himself too loudly,—as has since come to be the case with another great arranger of European strategy in another country. It was so. It is not within the compass of a man's nature to stretch his voice afar and yet to control the power of his own hand. Looking back, we can understand that Palmerston should have fallen; but we all feel that had he not risen to higher place because of his fall, England would have lost much by his falling.

In the autumn of 1850 General Haynau came to London, and, among other sights, visited Barclay & Perkins' brewery. According to English ideas he had shown himself to be a brute during the Hungarian war; and very brutally was he treated by the draymen. His name should not be mentioned here but that all England was in a momentary ferment because of what had been done. It was generally thought that he had been maltreated, and that, as he had not ill-used Englishmen or English women, we should have contented ourselves with simply ignoring him when he trusted himself to our hospitality. Palmerston's judgment as to what had been done was lenient. "The draymen were wrong in the particular course they adopted. Instead of striking him, which, however, by Koller's account, they did not do much, they ought to have tossed him in a blanket, rolled him in the kennel, and then sent him home in a cab, paying his fare to the hotel."

In his sixty-seventh year (January, 1851) he wrote to his brother from Broadlands. Speaking of the Christmas just past, he says; "I took a fling, and went out several days hunting and shooting in the fine of the early day, coming home, of course, for work earlier than if I had been only a sportsman." Let gentlemen of sixty-seven who habitually go out hunting and shooting,—for I am aware that there are Englishmen of the age who do so,—bethink themselves of the manner in which they pass the remainder of the day after they have come home. Are they tired, and do they sleep, or sit over their tea? Do they congratulate themselves that at sixty-seven they have been still able to perform so well many of the feats of their youth? I think I may say that they, none of them, betake themselves to the hard thoughtful work of their lives; and that, if such work still falls to their lot, it has to be done before they go out hunting or shooting.

He, however, takes his share in all matters of interest. He knows what is doing as to fortifications, and takes a strong interest in the subject. He writes to the Chancellor of the Exchequer; "Could you but take a sum, however small, to make a beginning, for similar defences at Plymouth?" He is very eager as to some system of volunteering. "Every other country that deserves to be called a power has this kind of reserved force." Then comes the great Exhibition of 1851,—the first of those marvellous palaces of industry which have since been studded thick over the world's surface. He is writing to Lord Normanby, and is speaking of the multitude. "The Queen, her husband, her eldest son and daughter, gave themselves in full confidence to this multitude, with no other guard than one of honour and the accustomed supply of stick-handed constables." And the Papacy has to be put down. "Our Papal Aggression Bill will be carried in spite of the opposition of the Irish members who are driven on by the influence of the priests over the Irish electors." As to this bill, however, I do not know that we are now inclined to take much pride to ourselves. Then Mr. Gladstone's Neapolitan letters were written, and so moved Naples, through England, that the Neapolitan prisons were at last opened. On this subject he tells an excellent story. "Walewski told Milnes the other day, as a proof of the goodness of heart of the King of Naples, that at his, Walewski's request, the King had at one time promised to set free three hundred prisoners against whom no charge or no proof had been established. 'How grateful,' said Milnes, 'these men must have been! Did they not come and thank you for their release?' 'Why,' said Walewski, 'you see, after the King had made the promise, the Chief of Police came to him, and said that if the men were set free he could not answer for the King's life. And so, you see, the men were not set free.'"

In November, 1851, we come to the cause of his fall,—which cause was in truth Napoleon's *Coup d'Etat*. The feeling in England, when the *Coup d'Etat* was first made known, was very averse to it. There was a belief that Napoleon had been guilty of falsehood and treachery. Mr. Kinglake, in his great work on the invasion of the Crimea, translates the words which Napoleon had used on the 13th of November, 1850—"The noblest object, and the most worthy of an exalted mind, is not to seek when in power how to perpetuate it, but to labour incessantly to fortify, for the benefit of all, those principles of authority and morality which defy the passions of mankind and the instability of laws." About a year after he had uttered this philanthropic but sententious idea he had filched the Empire. Englishmen did not like that; and though they were gradually won by the fealty of the Emperor to his English alliance so as to endure him, the stain of the falsehood still stuck to him through his twenty years of governing. Such we think has been the English feeling.

Such was not the feeling of Lord Palmerston, who knew more as to the state of Europe than any other Englishman, and was more keenly alive to the immediate needs of both France and England. He writes to Lord Normanby; "There is no other person at present competent to be at the head of affairs in France; and if Louis Napoleon should end by founding a dynasty, I do not see that we need regret it as far as English interests are concerned." "At all events, I say of Louis Napoleon, *laudo manentem*." But it was known that there had been private friendship between the two men while Louis Napoleon was living in England, and also that there had been a strong aversion on the part of Palmerston to the whole family of Bourbons. The Bourbons had during the entire period of his career, both before and after the coming of the Citizen King, ruled after that mysterious and crafty fashion which had produced at last the Spanish marriages. Palmerston no doubt desired something better than craft and mystery. The Bourbons had been expelled by the Revolution; but the Republic, as established with Louis Napoleon as its President, had not acted with much wisdom. To Palmerston's thinking something more nearly akin to the established rule of a dynasty was necessary for France,—and for England also if it was to remain in alliance with France,—than the wild and uninstructed enthusiasm of the Assembly. He did believe in Louis Napoleon, and continued no doubt to believe to the end of his life, justified, as he thought, by the French Emperor's early successes, and also by his friendship for England. He had left the world of politics before Napoleon had spun all his thread and run his reel out to the end. To me who write this, even the memory of the Emperor is distasteful. But the fall that was about to come upon Palmerston may have been in part due to his feeling for a man who stood higher in his estimation than in that of his countrymen. Years afterwards, in 1858, he had to retire with his Government, of which he was then the head, for a reason which was partly similar. We shall come to that before long; but it afforded another proof of the general tone of his mind towards Louis Napoleon.

Lord Normanby was our Ambassador in Paris; and from some cause, of which I know nothing, entertained different feelings. It may probably be that he, as an honest man, disliked the dishonesty of the President. There was a variance between him and Palmerston, and that too no doubt had its effect upon the coming circumstances. And it must be remembered that Lord Palmerston was already labouring under a sense of the disapprobation of his superior officers in that he would not submit his despatches in time for such surveillance as it was thought that they should receive. He had then against him at this moment the Prime Minister and his own Ambassador in Paris, who had been a Cabinet Minister, and the Court influence, and he had the feeling that he himself was on too friendly terms with the man who had achieved the *Coup d'Etat* by not the fairest means that ever were used in politics, and not by the cleanest instruments.

On the other hand, it must be borne in mind that Palmerston knew himself as few men do, and his own sagacity, and his general popularity in the country. His object was so to administer foreign affairs as might best redound to the honour of his country, and he was aware that there was no man in England who could teach him a lesson in that respect. As to his despatches, it was to him quite impracticable to encounter the required delay. There was an order to that effect, and other orders came. He, however, if he remained Foreign Secretary, must do so after his own fashion. But there arose at this moment another source of displeasure against him, which, joined to his disobedience as to the despatches, caused his dismissal.[H] Lord Palmerston had expressed to M. Walewski, who was then the Ambassador from France in London, his approbation of the *Coup d'Etat.* This assent had been given somewhat in an off-hand manner, so as not to have bound him absolutely to the words which he had used. He alleged that it was so. Count Walewski of course sent home to the new Emperor his report of the English Foreign Secretary's opinion.

Two days afterwards Palmerston instructed Lord Normanby as to his conduct; "I am commanded by her Majesty to instruct your Excellency to make no change in your relations with the French Government." And it seems that some ill-feeling was engendered in Paris by priority of the private to the official communication made. The private communication had been to the effect that Lord Palmerston entirely approved of what the President had done. It must be said that he did not admit having gone so far as this. He pointed out that Walewski had reported from memory the words spoken; that Turgot, the Minister in France, had reported the words verbally to Lord Normanby; and that Normanby had written home his remembrance of the anger which M. Turgot had expressed. M. Turgot was at loggerheads with Lord Normanby, M. Turgot representing the President-Emperor. "You need not at all trouble yourself to tell us 'what you are commanded by her Majesty to instruct me,' because we have known two days since what was our friend Lord Palmerston's opinion." It was thus that Turgot answered Lord Normanby,—with scorn added to acrimony, because Lord Normanby had ventured to suggest that had the English Government pleased, the English Government might have interfered with the French Government. Lord Normanby, in his official report, distinctly stated that he had made this communication to M. Turgot. But Lord Palmerston had never so instructed him; "I am commanded by her Majesty to instruct your Excellency to make no change in your relations with the French Government." There is no message contained in this, and these are Lord Palmerston's words; but Lord Normanby seems to have misunderstood them. At any rate the private communication had reached Paris first, and the official despatch two days afterwards. Then there were official and semi-angry despatches between the two Lords in London and Paris, and the question of which was right fell into the hands of Lord John Russell as Prime Minister.

The gravamen of the charge now made was that the Foreign Secretary, without the sanction of the Cabinet, had taken upon himself to tell the French Ambassador that the President-Emperor had done uncommonly well by arranging the *Coup d'Etat*. That readers should think that the President did very ill has nothing to do with the question. It is not alleged that there was disagreement in the Cabinet on that point,—though no doubt there was either in the Cabinet or without the Cabinet. This is simply a memoir of Lord Palmerston, and does not presume to be a vindication of his policy. And the present object is to show why he was dismissed, and how he turned upon those who had dismissed him, and got the better of them. He himself, in a letter written a few days later to his brother, gives a detailed history of the whole affair, in which he takes the trouble to show that as he had expressed himself to Walewski, so had other members of the Cabinet said the same thing to the same man at the same period; and he quotes Lord Lansdowne, and Charles Wood, and John Russell himself. Am I forbidden to do that which my colleagues did, what all London was doing,—that part of London who knew what they were talking about?

I will quote his own words, in which he tells his brother how he had defended himself to Lord John Russell. "I answered that his doctrine, so laid down, was new and not practical; that there is a well-known and perfectly understood distinction in diplomatic intercourse between conversations which are official and which bind Governments, and conversations which are unofficial and which do not bind Governments; that my conversation with Walewski was of the latter description, and that I said nothing to him which would in any degree or in any way fetter the action of the Government; and that if it was to be held that a Secretary of State could never express any opinion to a foreign Minister on passing events, except as the organ of a previously-consulted Cabinet, there would be an end of that easy and familiar intercourse which tends essentially to promote good understanding between Ministers and Governments." But as he goes on he expresses himself more warmly; "It is obvious that the reason assigned for my dismissal was a mere pretext, eagerly caught at for want of any good reason. The real ground was a weak truckling to the hostile intrigues of the Orleans family, Austria, Russia, Saxony, and Bavaria, and in some degree also of the present Prussian Government. All these parties found their respective views and systems of policy thwarted by the course pursued by the British Government, and they thought that if they could remove the Minister they would change the policy."

The "weak truckling" and the "hostile intrigues" I will lay aside, leaving it to the individual reader to judge of these expressions as he may please. But it is manifest that there were running at the time in Great Britain two currents as to foreign politics: the one which I can only define as English;—and the other, which I call the policy of absolutism, because I do not wish to descend to abuse, which I must do if I give to it any national name. That both were held with high patriotic ideas we should not doubt. Emperors and their Ministers naturally believe in Emperors and their Ministers. Those who are opposed to them are, to their thinking, a stubborn revolutionary crowd. If by little tricks the absolute party can gain a point in their own favour, a great stroke of policy is made. But they who maintain that the united opinion of the world at large may be best used for the governance of the world, may be as wise, and at any rate as honest, as their opponents. A comparison of the national success of nations is in their favour. Lord Palmerston, during his whole life after he had come to think of these things, and especially during the strongest part of his life in which he presided at the Foreign Office, held the British view, and would not allow himself to be driven from it for a moment. A constitutional king did not, as he thought, rule in the sense of holding the strings of national policy in his own hands. In defence of his view, he was authoritative, imperious, arrogant,—sometimes even tyrannical, if you will. The bull-dog can hardly hold tight by his bone without crushing it. But it is very difficult to get a bone out of the mouth of a bull-dog.[1]

When called upon for his explanation by Lord John, Lord Palmerston gave it, with more precision than accuracy. His letter is dated the 16th of December. He went at length into the question of the

President's conduct, and justified the President's judgment in the *Coup d'Etat*. But it was not that which was now called in question. There was a rejoinder made to him in which he was expected to acknowledge his error in having spoken to Walewski. This he refused to do, and then, on the 19th of December, there came the blow. Lord John wrote as follows; "I have just received your letter of yesterday. No other course is left to me than to submit the correspondence to the Queen, and to ask Her Majesty to appoint a successor to you in the Foreign Office." Lord Palmerston was dismissed. The dismissal of a Cabinet Minister, and of such a Cabinet Minister, was at any rate a most uncommon occurrence. It struck Lord Macaulay as "rashly, needlessly harsh." Lord John himself repented of it. "My own judgment upon it is, that it was hasty and precipitate," he says—page 258, of his "Recollections and Suggestions." He thought to soften the blow by offering to the dismissed, but ever active Secretary of State the *fainéant* retreat of Lord-Lieutenant of Ireland. One is almost tempted to think that Palmerston was right when in his earlier years he spoke of the average Minister as one who would "by instinct come round to the oat sieve."

He, however, would not come round after that fashion. He felt that it had been for some time intended that he should be dismissed; and, now that the blow had come, was by no means prepared to retire into obscurity and silence. But he seems to have experienced great difficulty in making up his mind how he would act. He did nothing;—nor was there anything to be done till Parliament should meet early in February. But it was, of course, manifest that Lord John should offer to the House his explanation of the most unwonted circumstance. This he did in a very powerful speech; but he could speak, knowing that the Court was at his back. Lord Palmerston answered him, but he did so without such backing; and could hardly have made his points good without a reference to the Court which his loyalty would forbid him to use. He seems to have recognized the fact that he must accept his dismissal, and bide his time, and try another fall with Lord John on other grounds. He knew his popularity with the country, and did not doubt his own power. Could he succeed on other ground, the Queen would be bound to accept him. A short time afterwards the Queen did accept him very willingly. But in his present difficulty even his popularity would not suffice to put him straight before the Parliament. It would not suit him, the old public servant of his country,—him who still hoped to serve his country long,—to take upon himself the rôle of a demagogue, and join as he must have joined the ultra-radicals in a vain endeavour to get a majority against his old chief. He made no effort of the kind, but allowed the matter to pass by, defending himself only on small points,—as to which it was not claimed for him by his friends that he was especially successful.

The debate was thus described by Lord Dalling, who was especially Palmerston's friend. "His speech,"—John Russell's—"certainly was one of the most powerful I ever heard delivered. It was evidently intended to crush an expected antagonist, and, by the details into which it went, took Lord Palmerston by surprise. I listened to his reply with the most affectionate interest, since he was kind enough to mention my own name with praise; but I felt, and all his friends felt, that it was feeble as a retort to the tremendous assault that had been made on him." "'Palmerston is smashed' was, indeed, the expression generally used at the clubs; but it did not in the least convey the idea that Lord Palmerston had formed of his own position. I must say, in truth, that I never admired him so much as at this crisis. He evidently thought he had been ill-treated; but I never heard him make an unfair or irritable remark, nor did he seem in anywise stunned by the blow he had received, or dismayed by the isolated position in which he stood." It was on this occasion that the witty Statesman expressed his opinion that "there was a Palmerston"—Fuit Ilium et ingens gloria Teucrorum. That Statesman intended to express his opinion that the power of Palmerston was a thing of the past.

"So sinks the daystar in the ocean bed,
And yet anon repairs his drooping head,
And tricks his beams, and with new-spangled ore
Flames in the forehead of the morning sky!"

❑❑❑

CHAPTER X

Palmerston Home Secrctary, 1853 and 1854

THE world had not to wait long. Lord Palmerston had, as we have seen, been turned out on the 19th of December, 1851. Parliament met on the 8th of February following, and before the month was over Lord John was out of office. A Militia Bill was brought in by him to which Palmerston expressed himself as antagonistic. It is not supposed that he had been anxious to turn out his late chief on that special question, but had rather selected it as a commencement for his attack; but the House reconsidered the matter on which Lord John had been triumphant, and supported the late Foreign Secretary so loudly by its cheers, as to make it apparent to the Head of the Government that he could no longer stand his ground. It was then that Palmerston wrote as follows to his brother;—"I have had my tit-for-tat with John Russell, and I turned him out on Friday last. I certainly, however, did not expect to do so, nor did I intend to do anything more than to persuade the House to reject his foolish plan and to adopt a more sensible one. I have no doubt that two things induced him to resign: first, the almost insulting manner towards him in which the House, by its cheers, went with me in the debate; and, secondly, the fear of being defeated on the vote of censure about the Cape affairs which was to have been moved to-day." Lord Palmerston speaks of Lord John's "foolish plan." It may probably be surmised that the abstract folly of the plan was not so potent with the writer of the letter as the determination of which he speaks "to have his tit-for-tat with John Russell." It cannot be but that personal questions in the bosoms of Statesmen should share the ground with matters of public import, and often lead to the forming of an opinion or the riveting of a doubt. If I hear of a public man with whom it has not been so, I feel that he must have lacked the warmth necessary for party conflict. "Measures not men," is a great war-cry by which to gain the voices of the ignorant; but, when they have been gained, men will count almost for as much as measures.

Lord Palmerston had at any rate delivered a knock-down blow, and Lord John was out. Lord Derby was sent for by the Queen, and in making his Cabinet offered to Lord Palmerston the place of Chancellor of the Exchequer. It was just forty-three years since the same place was offered him before, and then, as now, by a Tory Prime Minister. What a length of life to run between two such proposals! We are taught now to think that a man who first undertakes such duties as those of regulating the finances of his country at sixty-eight years of age, is taxing human nature too far; and certainly were we to hear that a youth of twenty-five had been so selected, we should think that he was very precocious, or that the Prime Minister was very silly. But this man refused both offers; and, without going into the motives which induced him to decline Lord Derby's proposition, we cannot but rejoice that he saw his way clearly to the refusal. We cannot but think that there would have been a drifting back to Toryism under Lord Derby which would have materially interfered with that popularity by which he was to be lifted up to the management of affairs during the Crimean War. In discussing with his brother the state of parties at the time, he thus says;—"The truth is that the Whigs would be glad to get rid of John Russell and to have me in his stead, if this change could well be accomplished." That, in truth, was the change which the Liberal party desired, without probably any defined expression of such a wish. The qualities of Lord Palmerston's mind had taken possession of men, and though the English Liberal of to-day would probably think twice before he would place the thoughtful statesmanship of the one below the happy audacity of the other, at the moment undoubtedly the country was tired of Lord John, and inclined to turn against him because he had turned out his old colleague.

No weaker Government than that of Lord Derby's was ever formed in England. The only persons in it well known at the time to political life were Lord Derby and Mr. Disraeli, who had fallen into the vacancy made by the death of a much weaker man than himself. Lord George Bentinck had gone, and left to Mr. Disraeli the leadership of the House of Commons. But when we look back over the not long interval of nineteen years we hardly know who they were that he had to lead. It has been said that besides Lord Derby and Mr. Herries there was not an English Privy Councillor among the number. It included none of Sir Robert Peel's followers. Free Trade was the one matter in dispute, and on the question of Free Trade there was a majority against Government consisting of Peelites, Whigs, and Radicals. Lord John and Lord Palmerston, together with Sir James Graham and Mr. Gladstone, declared it to be impossible to carry on the Government in such a condition of things. A new Parliament was called, and on the 11th of November, 1852, the Queen's Speech was read to them. Parliament was invited to consider whether recent legislation had not inflicted unavoidable injury.[J] This was intended as a direct slap in the face for the advocates of Free Trade. Mr. Villiers moved a counter-resolution, full, as Mr. Disraeli said, of "odious epithets." This was rejected by 336 votes to 256. Lord Palmerston then proposed a second resolution, declaring "That it is the opinion of the House that the improved condition of the people ... is mainly the result of recent legislation." This was directly at variance with the convictions of the Ministry, but it was accepted and allowed to pass by a great majority. The resolution is supposed to have been prepared by Sir James Graham, in concert with Lord John. And the fact of its adoption by Lord Palmerston, and its promotion by him in political concert with Lord John, proves that at this moment there was no war between the two old colleagues. The cause for war still remained, and did in fact prevent for the present any combination of Statesmen in which Lord Palmerston should serve under Lord John; but of personal quarrel there was none, and the two men were thus able to act together within twelve months of the day on which the fatal letter had been written. Lord Palmerston had in June of that year declared his purpose not to serve under Lord John. "He certainly has entirely lost mine." Lord John had lost Lord Palmerston's confidence. "I feel no resentment towards him personally or privately; but it would require strong inducements to persuade me to become again a member of a Government of which he was the head. I feel no confidence in his discretion or judgment as a political leader, and could place no trust in his steady fidelity as a colleague, having my official position at his mercy."

It was in vain, however, that Lord Derby accepted the resolution in favour of Free Trade. Mr. Disraeli brought in his Budget, which was at once thrown out by 303 votes to 286. This took place on the 16th of December, and on the 20th Lord Derby declared that the Ministry had resigned. Lord Aberdeen was then sent for, and formed the Administration in which Lord John Russell went in as Foreign Secretary and Lord Palmerston to the Home Office. There must have been to him in this a certain bitterness. He had at first declined Lord Aberdeen's offer because Lord Aberdeen's policy as Foreign Minister had for many years been at direct variance with his own. He had, however, been persuaded by Lord Lansdowne, who had been better able, perhaps, to read the signs of the times than could he himself, and the feelings of the minds of men towards him against whom the Court had used its influence. He was assured that the administration of Foreign Affairs would not rest with Lord Aberdeen, but with Lord Clarendon or Lord John,—and of the general liberality of both of these he was well assured. He says himself to his brother that he had determined that he himself would not in any case take the Foreign Office. In this, no doubt, there was some boasting,—natural and understood. It would have been impossible that Lord Palmerston should then have returned to the Foreign Office.

There is something almost ludicrous in the energy displayed by Lord Palmerston at the Home Office; and yet it was essentially useful. He visited prisons and wrote memoranda on the ventilation of cells.

He arranged tickets-of-leave for convicts, and attempted to abate the nuisance of smoke in London. He built cemeteries, and fixed the winter assizes. Such matters are by no means ludicrous. It is by attending to them that the welfare of a people is in a great measure obtained. They are, no doubt, as important as those foreign arrangements for the government of Europe,—and, indeed, of the world at large,—in which Lord Palmerston had been hitherto engaged. But they do not loom so large before the imagination. And we can imagine that he himself felt the difference when he descended from instructing Sir Stratford Canning to consulting a factory inspector.

It was about this time, I think, that he fell into a habit of intercourse with the public generally which adhered to him till the day of his death. He became notorious as a joker. He passed on from the light, courteous *persiflage* of the Foreign Minister to the common John-Bull fun of an English magistrate, without an apparent effort, but with an evident intention. The wit was never very good. It must be acknowledged that it was generally commonplace, and that from the mouth of another it would have had no effect. But the world had so come to love its Palmerston that it was ready to laugh at everything; and when the world of deputations has been made to laugh, much has been achieved. The deputations did laugh, and Lord Palmerston obtained the character of being the wittiest Englishman of his day. No character was ever more cheaply earned, or used to a better effect.

Looking back at these days, we seem to remember that Lord Palmerston, as Home Secretary, appeared larger to us than did other Ministers of the day. He was not only Home Secretary, but had confided to him the duty of general adviser in public matters. The great trouble of the Crimean War was coming on, and the state of things was not so well known to others as to him. There was, too, a question as to Reform, regarding which he all but felt himself compelled to resign. "My office is too closely connected with Parliamentary changes to allow me to sit silent during the whole progress of a Reform Bill through Parliament; and I could not take up a Bill which contained material things of which I disapprove, and assist to fight it through the

House of Commons, to force it on the Lords, and to stand upon it at the hustings." This he said in a letter to his brother-in-law, Lawrence Sulivan. We can understand that, for the satisfaction of his own political feelings, he need not have stirred himself much on any question of Reform. But it must have been difficult for him to have a Reform Bill settled for him while he was Home Secretary. There was, too, a double reason for his disagreement at the moment. Should the fleet move up to the Dardanelles, or should it remain in the Mediterranean? This was in anticipation of that which afterwards became the Crimean War, and was a matter on which Lord Palmerston was likely to have a more decided opinion than in regard to the Reform Bill. But at last he withdrew his resignation. "I remain in the Government. I was much and strongly pressed to do so for several days by many of the members of the Government, who declared that they were no parties to Aberdeen's answer to me, and that they considered all the details of the intended Reform measure as still open to discussion. Their earnest representations and the knowledge that the Cabinet had on Thursday taken a decision on Turkish affairs in entire accordance with opinions which I had long unsuccessfully pressed upon them, decided me to withdraw my resignation, which I did yesterday."

This was at the close of 1853, when Parliament was not sitting, and for the next two years the Crimean War became so completely the one matter of vital interest to England as to make it necessarily the point on which a memoir of Lord Palmerston's life for those two years must altogether hang. He was Home Secretary when the war began, but had been lifted up to the position of Prime Minister before its close. This was done that England might be able to have, as she ought, the most competent man she possessed to conduct it for her. I am not expressing an opinion that he was the most competent man,—only that England so thought, and justified her opinion by the final result. But in truth the capability of a man for such work does not depend on any power of intellect, or indomitable courage, or far-seeing cunning. The man is competent simply because he is believed to be so. A nation trusts a man, and will go to work under him in a manner which is impossible for it to adopt under a leader that it does not trust. And, as seems to be the case with all men who are brought into a difficult operation, and succeed in it, just at the moment convenient for success, Lord Palmerston took the matter in hand exactly at the right time. It may be that Aberdeen had failed because he was Aberdeen, and Palmerston succeeded because he was Palmerston, each by such lights and gifts as were in him. That was, and still is, the average Englishman's idea. Or it may be that Palmerston, with his usual luck, stepped in just when the evil days were over and success was becoming possible. That is the idea of clever critics of affairs. Who shall say which was correct?

We must go back here, and in the slightest possible manner touch upon the causes of the great war. They had had their beginning while Lord Palmerston was at the Foreign Office, even if they be not said to have commenced earlier than that. The nominal cause was a dispute which grew up in Jerusalem between the Latin and the Greek Churches for possession of the highest authority over the Holy Places. It was acknowledged that the Holy Places should be open to both, but it was considered essential that one should be supreme. It need hardly be said that with this contest England had no personal concern. It was settled at last by the perplexed Turk on the advice of the English Ambassador. But it was so settled as to make Nicholas, the Emperor of Russia, more convinced than ever of the general necessity of taking all the members of the Greek Church in Turkey especially under his protection. This he attempted to do in the fulness of autocratic authority. Then, when demur was made to the Emperor's claim, Count Mentschikoff was sent across the Pruth so as to occupy the Danubian Principalities, which, as far as this transaction was concerned, were at the time a part of Turkey. All Europe at once went to work to induce him to return. England, France, Austria, and Prussia, at any rate, did so. But Nicholas, who had long been busy and greedy over the chattels of the "sick man," would not retire without achieving something. And Turkey, thoroughly supported by that famous Englishman, Sir Stratford Canning,—who had now become Lord Stratford de Redcliffe,—would grant him nothing in the way of a protectorate. A conference met at Vienna, with a pundit from each of the four countries, to save Turkey, and at the same time to save if possible the feelings and the honour of the Czar. But the attempt came to nothing, and was at last altogether abortive.

Mr. Kinglake seems to attribute to Lord Palmerston almost more than a friendly compliance with Napoleon in this matter. "There was not, perhaps, more than one member of the English Cabinet who desired the formation of this singular alliance on grounds like those which moved the French Emperor." We presume that Lord Palmerston was the Cabinet Minister here indicated. Again he says; "Of the bulk of the Cabinet, and possibly of all of them except one, Lord Clarendon's pithy phrase was the true one. They drifted" (vol. i. p. 440). Napoleon probably was anxious to obtain for himself the *éclat* of going to war with Queen Victoria for his ally. For a man who had obtained his empire as he had done it was a great thing to appear before the world with such a Sovereign for his friend. We can understand that in fighting Russia he should be actuated by such a motive. But the Coup d'Etat had taken place in the winter of 1851-1852, and the pundits were at their work of peace in Vienna during the summer of 1853. The dates do not hold good for the continuance of such a project on the part of Napoleon. It might have served for three months to keep his throne, but could hardly have been serviceable after fifteen. We do know that Lord Aberdeen was weak, doing his best to stave off war if he could do so. And we know also that Palmerston was strong, anxious from the beginning to act in accordance with the English Ambassador at Constantinople. But we doubt whether there be reason to suppose that he had lent himself to the wishes of the Emperor of the French, or desired to go beyond his own Ambassador.

Looking back at the whole character of the man through a long life, we find that his fault has been that of confident,—almost that of self-opinionated audacity. Having the advantage of his private correspondence,—which had not been revealed to Mr. Kinglake when his first volumes were published,—we can read in it no trace of such friendship, or, we may say, of such anti-British feeling. He was ready to fight any man who was not an Englishman for any point,—and any man who was an Englishman who opposed him, as long as he had a leg to stand upon. I am inclined, therefore, to think that Palmerston, in his readiness for war with Russia, was in no degree guided by imperial sympathies. In July he wrote as follows to Lord Aberdeen; "I quite agree with you that we ought to try whether we can devise any proposal which, without involving any departure by the Sultan from the ground of independence on which he has taken his stand, might satisfy any just claim which the Emperor can put forward. In the meantime, however, I hope you will allow the squadrons to be ordered to go up to the Bosphorus as soon as it is known in Constantinople that the Russians have entered the Principalities, and to be further at liberty to go into the Black Sea, if necessary or useful for the protection of Turkish territory." And he ends his letter as follows; "I am confident that this country expects that we should pursue such a course, and I cannot believe that we should receive anything but support in pursuing it from the party in Opposition." Then he writes to Lord John Russell; "In my opinion, the course which the Emperor"—the Emperor of Russia,—"has pursued on these matters from his first overtures for a partition of Turkey, and especially the violent, abusive, and menacing language of his last manifesto, seem to show that he has taken his line, and that nothing will satisfy him but complete submission on the part of Turkey; and we ought, therefore, not to disguise from ourselves that he is bent upon a stand-up fight."

"I tried again to persuade the Cabinet to send the squadrons up to the Bosphorus, but failed; I was told that Stratford and La Cour have powers to call for them. This is, no doubt, stated in public despatches, but we all know that he has been privately desired not to do so. Words may properly be answered by words, but acts should be replied to by acts; and the entrance of the Russians as invaders into the Turkish territory ought to be followed and replied to by the entrance of the squadrons into the Bosphorus as protectors." Here Palmerston seems to speak with his wonted voice. It was as though the foreign affairs of England were all but under his control. It may be that he and the Emperor of the French were of one mind. Or it may be that the Emperor, knowing which way Palmerston was inclined to lead, foresaw that he could best play his own part by walking with him. But of the two men we think it probable that Lord Palmerston knew Eastern Europe the better, and had the clearer idea of what he intended to do. Still in July, he writes thus to the members of the Cabinet; "The Russian Government has been led on step by step by the apparent timidity of the Government of England; and reports, artfully propagated that the British Cabinet had declared that it would have *la paix à tout prix*, have not been sufficiently contradicted by any overt acts." But Lord Aberdeen was instinctively against the war into which, as Lord Clarendon afterwards said, England had drifted, and Lord Clarendon, who had become Foreign Secretary, agreed with Lord Aberdeen.

It must be remembered that the Emperor Nicholas was thoroughly convinced that England, and especially England under the guidance of Lord Aberdeen, would not allow herself to be driven into war. He read the speeches in the House of Commons, and probably counted even the votes. To the English money-making commercial mind, war he conceived to be of all things the most antipathetic. Looking forward as well as his intellect would allow him, he thought he saw that the British power was in her decline. Sir Stratford Canning and Lord Palmerston he had always hated. They were two special foes; but they were only two. All England, with her bales of cotton, would certainly not go to war. Such was the conviction of the Emperor Nicholas. And, since Lord Aberdeen had come into power at the preceding Christmas, such also had been the tendency of the English Prime Minister's mind. But the will of Lord Palmerston,—and the will also of the Emperor of the French,—had been stronger than that of Lord Aberdeen. Very much in compliance with Palmerston's instructions, the two fleets did pass up the Dardanelles on the 14th of October, and were brought to an anchor immediately off Constantinople. The two Lords in the English Cabinet were still hardly acting in concert, though Lord Aberdeen's nature was so gracious as to make actual opposition to his colleague almost impossible. He, too, had at his back the Prince Consort, who, though he agreed to war under certain circumstances, was not of one mind with Lord Palmerston as to what those circumstances were.[K] Lord Palmerston defines his ideas in the following words; "We passed the Rubicon when we first took part with Turkey, and sent our squadrons to support her; and when England and France have once taken a third Power by the hand, that third Power must be carried in safety through the difficulties in which it may be involved. England and France cannot afford to be baffled, and whatever measures may be necessary on their part to baffle their opponent, those measures must be adopted; and the Governments of the two most powerful countries on the face of the earth must not be frightened, either by words or things, either by the name or by the reality of war." That was dated on the 1st of November, hardly a clear month before Sinope, and indicates what were then his intentions.

When the fleets had passed up the Dardanelles, the anger of Nicholas was very great. He had never thought that by crossing the Pruth he had given a *casus belli*; and as without such provocation the passage of the fleets up to Constantinople would have been an infraction of a well-understood treaty, he considered himself to have been grossly insulted and misused. Was it the fact that these English did intend to fight him? He was a Sovereign who had made awful preparations for war, and he was aware that the English army was, in these latter days, always maintained on a peace-footing,—what to him must have appeared a cheap and nasty military arrangement. If these English attempted to follow up their fleet, he would let them feel the weight of his right hand. But it was incumbent on him, at any rate, to punish the Turks. Therefore he sent his own fleet out from Sebastopol, and arranged matters for Sinope.

The reader must remember that during this time Lord Palmerston was Secretary of State for Home Affairs, and was by no means specially called upon to attend to this Russo-Turkish question. He had his smoke and his cemeteries, and his factories and his law courts, to look after.

❑❑❑

CHAPTER XI

The Crimean War;—Palmerston Prime Minister, 1855

THE war began in earnest with the naval conflict at Sinope. It was a terrible deed, and done, we must say, altogether in revenge. The English and French fleets had gone up the Dardanelles, and by doing so had offended the proud nature of Nicholas past all immediate forgiveness. The Russian ships came out from Sebastopol, and, after hovering about the Black Sea for a fortnight, to see, probably, whether the combined fleet would interfere, and finding that the small Turkish squadron lying at Sinope was at their mercy, went in and destroyed it altogether. "It was believed by men in authority," says Mr. Kinglake, "that 4,000 Turks were killed, and that less than 400 survived, and that all these were wounded."[L]

England was full of wrath, and nothing would appease her anger but a conviction that now, let the Prime Minister say what he would, we should fight Russia. Looking back on the circumstance over many years, we must acknowledge that the Emperor of Russia had on his side any legal rights which a state of war can give. He, out of his own mad sense of power, had crossed the Pruth, and we,—the French, that is, and ourselves,—had on the part of our allies taken our fleets up to Constantinople. The Russians had returned back across the Pruth; but Nicholas refused to say that he would give up his idea of a protectorate. The allies had therefore gone with their fleets into the Black Sea, and there could be no doubt that a state of war existed. But the Russian

Admiral had six or seven ships of the line on the spot, whereas the Turks had but seven frigates. There was no hope for them, but still they fought bravely while they had a gun to fight, and perished at last almost to a man. Our fleet, the meanwhile, was lying at the Bosphorus, and all England was angry. Nothing but war could now serve to quiet the minds of Englishmen.

On the 10th of December, 1853, Lord Palmerston wrote to the Prime Minister, recommending that we in England should at once prepare to fight;—"What I would strongly recommend, therefore, is that which I proposed some months ago to the Cabinet, namely, that the Russian Government and the Russian Admiral at Sebastopol should be informed that so long as Russian troops occupy the Principalities, or hold a position in any other part of the Turkish territory, no Russian ships of war can be allowed to show themselves out of port in the Black Sea." Lord Aberdeen declined the advice thus given, and on the 15th Lord Palmerston resigned. But the Government could not go on without him. "In truth," says Mr. Kinglake, "he was gifted with the instinct which enables a man to read the heart of a nation."[M] He was no sooner gone than the Cabinet in his absence did decide upon sending the fleet into the Black Sea; and then the resignation was withdrawn. Lord Aberdeen wrote to him as follows;—"I am glad to find that you approve of a recent decision of the Cabinet with respect to the British and French fleets, adopted in your absence. I feel sure you will have learnt with pleasure that, whether you are absent or present, the Government are duly careful to preserve from all injury the interests and dignity of the country." On the 7th of February the Russian Ambassador was recalled, and troops were immediately sent to the East. Then there was a dinner given to Sir Charles Napier at the Reform Club, for which Lord Palmerston was held to be specially responsible. It was not, perhaps, done in the best taste or with the most correct judgment. A triumphant banquet to a conquering hero should follow, and not precede, the victories to be celebrated. Lord Palmerston presided, and was very triumphant and very jocund. He told stories of all that the Admiral had done in the Mediterranean and elsewhere, and suggested all that he would do in the Baltic. Mr. Bright fell very foul of him, and perhaps deservedly. Lord Palmerston retorted on Mr. Bright with severity, and a considerable amount of ill-feeling was engendered. Mr. Bright belonged then, as now, to the Peace party, and found an ample scope for attack in the loud joy of a Minister who was exciting his fellow-countrymen to war; and, undoubtedly, he had the best of it in the end, as Sir Charles did not return triumphant.

The British troops now flocked into Turkey, and the transit across from Varna to the Crimean Peninsula was quickly achieved. On the 14th of September the first detachments of the English and French armies landed, and a few days later the battle of the Alma was fought and won. We can still remember the feeling of triumph with which the news was heard, and the spirit of conquest which was enhanced by the false tidings, believed at the time, that Sebastopol also had fallen. England did think for a few hours that she had already done that which was to cost her twelve months of heart-rending anxieties, many millions of taxes, and woe beyond measure. Hitherto, as we have read the records of the preparations for the campaign, it has appeared that Lord Palmerston, as Home Secretary, has had more to do with the war than any other Minister. But he escaped the personal annoyance to which those were subjected who had the management of the details in their hands, and who were supposed to be responsible for what was amiss. But the time was soon to come in which he would cease to be an underling;—and then, such was his luck, all things went well.

After the battle of the Alma things did not go prosperously. England, when she was brought back from the feeling of triumph which had almost overpowered her on the false report of the fall of Sebastopol, expected that though the stronghold had not yet fallen into her hands, it should be made to do so very quickly. She was unreasonable in the severity with which she treated her servants, both civil and military, at home and in the Crimea. England, not being accustomed to war on a great scale for the last forty years, could not at first carry it on as though she were used to it, and accused all her servants of "routine," "red tape," blundering, and ignorance. We can look back now and see that such were the charges made by the austere mistress, and remember the names of Lord Raglan and the Duke of Newcastle with affection and respect, though we broke the heart of the one and the spirit of the other by our usage. But if the servants are noble-minded, as is generally the case with English servants in high places, even when broken-hearted, they leave examples behind them which instigate others to renewed efforts.

When the tidings of failures came Lord John Russell was himself the first to declare that his own colleague at the War Department was unfit for his position. That colleague was the unfortunate Duke of Newcastle, and Lord John recommended that "before Parliament meets Lord Palmerston should be entrusted with the seals of the War Department." Lord Aberdeen, however, declined to dismiss the Duke of Newcastle, and then Mr. Roebuck moved for the appointment of a Select Committee to inquire into the condition of our army. Lord John immediately resigned, by no means with the good-will of his colleagues. Lord John had been leader of the House, and on his desertion the defence of Lord Aberdeen and of the Duke of Newcastle was left to Lord Palmerston. He said, which was true enough, that our misfortunes had come from the inexperience caused by a long peace. The House divided on Mr. Roebuck's motion, and the Ministry were defeated by a great majority. It was found that 305 members followed Mr. Roebuck into the lobby against only 148, who supported the Government. It was clear, at any rate, that Lord Aberdeen must resign.

But though Lord Palmerston must resign also with his chief, and appeared for the time as the second in command of a beaten army, it was to him a moment of great triumph. There was no longer a question whether he should again serve under Lord John or with Lord John, or whether he should be compelled on behalf of his country to serve under one whose general politics were so distasteful to him as those of Lord Aberdeen. Lord Derby was at once invited to form a Government,—but in vain. He applied to Lord Palmerston to help him; but it was not thus, we can fancy, that Lord Palmerston saw his way through the future troubles. Lord Derby could well understand that if he were to be a successful Prime Minister in a War Cabinet, he must have Lord Palmerston as his right-hand man. But it was not so long since this same Lord Derby, then Lord Stanley, had brought against him in the House of Lords the bitterness of the Don Pacifico arraignment. It was not that this would have stood in Palmerston's way, had it been possible for him to have thrown his heart into the work in conjunction with Lord Derby. But such a conjunction cannot be always attained by mere volition. Political coalitions are never firm, because they are formed of individual men, and each man has a heart in his bosom in which he carries his memories of the past as well as his hopes for the future. "I have come to the conclusion," he said, "that if I were to join your Government, as proposed by you, I should not give to that Government that strength which you are good enough to think would accrue to you from my acceptance of office." Lord John was then sent for, and made the attempt. Lord Clarendon and others of the party would not serve with him, though Lord Palmerston had consented to do so. Lord John, in telling Lord Palmerston of his failure, offered to serve with him, should the Queen require his services. There was no other alternative. Indeed there was no other man than Lord Palmerston in England who could have carried on the war. The Queen sent for him, and Lord John did join him.

" ... Quod optanti Divûm promittere nemo
Auderet, volvenda dies en attulit ultro."

It was thus he signified his final triumph to his brother,—or intended so to signify it, but quoted the passage wrongly.

There is in this a boyish feeling of the happiness of success. And yet he was seventy years old. We cannot fancy such an expression coming from Lord John or Lord Aberdeen. Though either had felt it, he could not have so written to his brother. Here I am at last,—Prime Minister of England, in spite of all accidents. My old friend, Lord John, turned me out of the Foreign Office the other day. And I was obliged to go at his bidding. And I had a bad quarter of an hour in the House of Commons when, for reasons which are always paramount with an Englishman, I was unable to take my own part.

They said I was crushed. "There was a Palmerston." But when these times of war had come, I was wanted, And now my Lord John is my lieutenant. All that was not loudly expressed in the "volvenda dies en attulit ultro;" but it was understood both by the writer and by his brother. And he goes on: "Here am I, writing to you from Downing Street as First Lord of the Treasury. The fact was, that Aberdeen and Newcastle had become discredited in public estimation as Statesmen equal to the emergency; Derby felt conscious of the incapacity of the greater portion of his party, and their unfitness to govern the country; and John Russell, by the way in which he suddenly abandoned the Government, had so lost caste for the moment that I was the only one of his political friends who was willing to serve under him." "I think our Government will do very well. I am backed by the general opinion of the whole country, and I have no reason to complain of the least want of cordiality or confidence on the part of the Court." Lord Aberdeen had himself done his best to make the matter easy for Lord Palmerston. I quote the following words from the "Life of the Prince Consort" (vol. iii. p. 209);—"Lord Palmerston had good reason to appreciate the generosity with which his old chief had interposed to remove this formidable impediment to his success." Nor was Her Majesty less grateful; and in her letter, 6th of February, announcing to Lord Aberdeen that Lord Palmerston had just kissed hands upon his appointment as Premier, she told him that she was now relieved from great anxiety and difficulty, and felt that she owed much to Lord Aberdeen's kind and disinterested assistance. Then he states the terms which he intends to propose to the enemy, and in doing so prophesies the future almost exactly. "We must also *ask* for the destruction of the works at Sebastopol, although we should not make that a *sine quâ non* unless we had taken the place and had destroyed the works ourselves."

A majority of the House of Commons, led by Mr. Roebuck, and with the people of the country to back them, insisted on inquiry, on punishment, on improvement, and increased activity. We still remember how "red tape" and "routine" were in all our mouths. Mail after mail brought home news of increased suffering. Palmerston had become

Prime Minister in February, 1855, and it was during the winter then drawing to its close that the sufferings and struggles of the Army had been most intense. Balaclava had been fought in October; the battle of Mount Inkerman in November; the great storm was on the 14th of that month; and, as the winter wore on, tidings of the difficulties of transit from Balaclava to the heights reached us,—and at last the road was made. It was in the middle of all these difficulties that Palmerston had become Prime Minister, and that Mr. Roebuck urged on his committee. Sir James Graham, Mr. Gladstone, and Mr. Sydney Herbert then retired; but others came in their places, and Lord Palmerston still went on; and during all the misery of the time,—for England was miserable with the sense of failure, or, at least, of performance not perfected,—he never quailed, or expressed any diffidence as to the work to which he had been called. It was the nature of the man not to be diffident, and therefore he succeeded. His courage was coarse and strong and indomitable, like that of a dog. We should say that he never trembled, even when he laid his head upon his pillow, because of the task imposed upon him. He would go on, having England at his back, and did not doubt but that the country would be found standing on its legs when the struggle should come to an end. I do not know that there was any one concerned in the matter whose heart was exactly of the same calibre. It was the very type of health, unadorned,—as also unalloyed,—by romance or high feeling, or poetry, or even sentiment.

In the midst of these things, in the early spring, the Emperor Nicholas died,—died broken-hearted, a victim to his own pride; but the contest went on the same as ever.

A second conference, to which Lord John went on the part of England, was held at Vienna, to arrange, if possible, the terms of peace, and to fix the four principal headings,—the condition of the Principalities, the navigation of the Danube, the power which Russia was to assume, or not to assume, in the Black Sea, and the independence of the Porte. In his operations there Lord John was held by the country to have failed. Indeed, he had never really succeeded in any political effort since the day on which he had ventured to dismiss

Lord Palmerston. And yet Lord Palmerston had been true to him. Lord Palmerston had never opposed him since the great blow by which he had turned him out on the Militia Bill. In truth, the people had not been with him, and had ceased to trust him. But to the other man the people had been true throughout. Lord Palmerston had no capability for thought equal to that of which Lord John was the master; but he possessed an instinctive sympathy with the masses which supported him to the end of his days.

The Vienna Conference was broken up, but the war still was carried on, certainly with the most exemplary care on the part of the septuagenarian Prime Minister. He writes as follows to Lord Panmure, the Minister for War;—"This is capital news from the Sea of Azoff, and the extensive destruction of magazines and supplies in the towns attacked must greatly cripple the Russian army in the Crimea. I am very sorry, however, to see so sad an account of the health of the Sardinians, and I strongly recommend you to urge Raglan, by telegraph to-day, to move the Sardinian camp to some other and healthier situation. Such prevalence of disease as the telegraphic message mentions must be the effect of some local cause." "As the cholera seems to be increasing among the troops, I should advise you to send for the doctor I mentioned." "We are 40,000 men short of the number voted by Parliament, and we shall be without the shadow of an excuse if we do not resort to every possible means and every possible quarter to complete our force to the number which Parliament has authorized." "Do not forget to suggest to our commissariat people in the Black Sea that large supplies of oxen to be eaten, and of horses to be ridden and to draw, may be derived from the country on the eastern shore of the Sea of Azoff." "It would be well also to point their attention to the projecting neck of land or island called Krassnoi, in the Bay of Perekop, which is said to abound in sheep and hay." From these quotations it will be seen how sleepless was his watchfulness, and how minute his attentions to the affairs of the war. He writes to his brother in August of the same year, and speaks of the probable fall of Sebastopol. "Our danger will then begin—a danger of peace, and not a danger of war." "I must try to fight the battle of negotiation as well as the battle of war, and, fortunately, the spirit of the English nation will support us. I wish I could reckon with equal confidence on the steady determination of the French."

In September Sebastopol had fallen, and the difficulties did in truth begin. He had now to contend not only with Russia, but with Austria and also with France. It is said of course that his spirit of contention was simply interference, and that in all things he wrote and spoke as a bully. It is difficult indeed to defend his manner; but that which he desired to get, he desired honestly. He desired it always on behalf of his country, and he usually got it. He writes as follows in January, 1856, to our Ambassador at Vienna;—"My dear Seymour,—Buol's statement to you the night before last was what, in plain English, we should call impertinent. We are happily not yet in such a condition that an Austrian minister should bid us sign a treaty without hesitation or conditions. The Cabinet of Vienna, forsooth, must insist upon our doing so! Why, really our friend Buol must have had his head turned by his success at St. Petersburg, and quite forgot whom he was addressing such language to." "We know the exhaustion, the internal pressure, difficulties, and distress of Russia quite as well as Buol does; but we know better than he does our own resources and strength. He may rest assured, however, that we have no wish to continue the war for the prospect of what we may accomplish another year, if we can now obtain peace upon the conditions which we deem absolutely necessary and essential; but we are quite prepared to go on if such conditions cannot be obtained. The British nation is unanimous in this matter. I say unanimous, for I cannot reckon Cobden, Bright, and Co. for anything." And he was right. The British nation did support him, and, in spite of Mr. Cobden and Mr. Bright, would have supported no minister who had acted otherwise. The Emperor of the French, now that the war was over,—now rather when it was possible to bring it to an end,—was desirous of softening the terms for Russia. But England was not specially desirous,—was not in a hurry. England was better able to continue the fight than she had been to begin it, and was by no means willing to give up any of those points for which she had expended her blood and her money. It had cost her fifty millions and 25,000 men. Having paid so dearly for her whistle, she was determined to have as much of it as might be possible. Therefore it must, I think, be admitted, that Lord Palmerston, in his arrogance, showed no more than the concentrated essence of an Englishman. It may be said that the feeling of the country was bulldog, turbulent, arrogant, and headstrong; but it was honest, and in all that it did it was guided by the feeling that each man should have that which was properly his own.

It would be vain in such a memoir as this to go back to the question of the right or wrong of the Crimean War. Lord Clarendon wittily declared that we had "drifted" into it. The word has been considered happy, and, since our passion on the subject has been over, has been used extensively to indicate our own folly in the matter. But if we had not gone to war, together with our French allies, would not Nicholas have been allowed to drift into Constantinople? It has been one of the chief efforts of Europe in the present century to restrain the ambition of the Czar of Russia. Whether this has or has not been a wise desire need not be discussed here. But it will, I think, be admitted, that when the Emperor's troops had crossed the Pruth and occupied a position on Turkish territory, they would not have receded without doing something on their master's behalf—unless they had been made to do so. Lord Aberdeen had thought that they could be made to go back by the force of argument. And the Czar had thought that he need not go back without gaining some portion of his road to Constantinople, because Lord Aberdeen's thoughts had been of so peaceful a nature. Therefore Lord Palmerston was put into Lord Aberdeen's place, and the Czar had to go back—with terrible consequences to himself. How it might have ended had the English people been less turbulent and headstrong, it would require a wise man to say. But had not Palmerston been there to their hand, some other Prime Minister would have been found to do the work, and to do it probably with less skill in the management.

The feelings of England with regard to Turkey, and also in regard to Russia, have changed since the Crimean War. And there has been reason for the change. At that time it had been the intention of the Emperor Nicholas gradually to swallow the Sultan's dominions,—to swallow them, or to have them swallowed by some other confederate and hungry animal. We all remember, as though it were yesterday, the proposal for the partition of the sick man's goods. The suggestion did not suit us. But as we would have none of these goods for ourselves, neither would we permit another to take them. We felt that for us Russia would be a more dangerous occupant of the Eastern Mediterranean than Turkey. And though we thought but little of the Mahommedan, we thought almost less of the Russian Christian. It was, at any rate, indispensable for our purposes that the Turk should be maintained. The half of the population of Turkey in Europe were Christians, whom we thought to be as near to civilization as the Muscovite from further North; and we flattered ourselves that it might be possible for us to teach them and their Mahommedan compatriots some touch of better manners. With the Russian we conceived that we could do nothing. There was much of mistaken vanity in this, because we had told ourselves that this people, thoroughly averse to us in customs, might be tamed and reduced and made like ourselves by the execution of a few treaties and the loan of a good deal of money. They took our money, and increased their harems, and laughed at our treaties. But still we had gained our object in this, that the Turk and not the Russian owned, and was likely to own, Constantinople. We had beaten back the Russian, to whom, though we did not begrudge him the power to increase his borders in Asia,—except in our own special direction,—we did refuse any advance in Europe. With these ideas, and on this theory, we went to war, and as we were by treaty the joint protectors of Turkey, the war was surely justifiable. Whether we got a good investment for our fifty millions, and, also, for our 25,000 English lives, is a question which we cannot now settle. The way in which it is settled by each individual depends on his own occupation in life. Does he breed cattle, or does he make carpets?

But in the quarter of a century which has passed since the Crimean War the Turk has done very much to make the blood of an Englishman boil. We lent him money on the promise of certain performances. He has spent our money, but has performed none of his promises. We have called upon him again and again to reform, and he has replied by expressing his desire for more money. He has done nothing to change his habits, and has only proved to us that a Mahommedan Turk cannot become a good Christian.

And this is the man for whom we expended 25,000 lives in war and fifty millions in war expenses, for which we have no claim on any one,—and many other millions in loans, as to which it would be better for our peace of mind if also we had no claim! The Mahommedan must certainly be made to go out of Europe, but it must be by slow degrees, and not at the instance of a despotic Emperor, who, under the name of a religious protectorate, would take possession of the country. Let any one who is still unhappy on the score of Turkey take the modern map of Europe, and compare the lines as they are drawn now and as they were drawn sixty years ago. He will see that the banishment of the Turk has not been so very slow.

Not, therefore, from dislike to Turkish rule should the English reader decide that the war into which he will have been told we had drifted, was inexpedient or more expensive than has been justified by the objects attained. That war was essentially one of Lord Palmerston's making. He advised it, commenced it, carried it on, and completed it. His hand—instant, urgent, and pressing—is to be seen in it throughout. We cannot yet say that it was all wise. It may well be that the world shall never be able to say with any certainty whether it was wise or foolish; but as far as the world has gone yet, no verdict has been given against it.

❑❑❑

CHAPTER XII

The Indian Mutiny

ON the 12th of July, 1856, at the Court at Buckingham Palace, Lord Palmerston was made a Knight of the Garter, it being understood that this was done in recognition of his services in reference to the Crimean War. When we remember what had occurred a few years back as to his dismissal from the Foreign Office, we may allow that he was bound to accept this token of her Majesty's favour. Lord Melbourne is reported to have said some years earlier, when a similar opportunity had come to him, that he had no need to bribe himself;—and he died without having K.G. written after his name. It is probable that no such word was used by Lord Melbourne, and that the cynical phrase was one merely made to suit the occasion. But there was a truth in it which took hold of men. There is, perhaps, a feeling that, as the Prime Minister is supposed to recommend the recipients of this honour for Her Majesty's acceptance, Palmerston would not now stand lower in the world's esteem had he declined it. Lord Fortescue, who was installed on the same day, could well afford to accept the blue ribbon. There was a reason why Lord Palmerston should accept it. But had he not done so, there would have been an increased glory in going to his rest, as Lord Melbourne had done, without burdening his name with the additional title.

In August, 1856, when Lord Palmerston was surrounded by the difficulties incident to the completion of the war, he lost his only brother; and with him those letters came to an end, which give us the freest account of Lord Palmerston's thoughts, his ambition, his arrogance, and his justice. We do not hear a word from him afterwards about his brother. He might have been the merest casual friend, chance-selected for some smaller embassy. For his elder brother had never pushed him up to the higher places at Paris, Constantinople, Vienna, or St. Petersburg. Sir William Temple had probably lacked something either in intellect or energy, or perhaps in discretion, of that fitness for the duties of an ambassador which had been found in Lord Granville, Sir Stratford Canning, and Sir Hamilton Seymour. At any rate Lord Palmerston was determined that he would not be accused of nepotism. In expressions of grief there is somewhat of feminine feeling, which, to the nature of Lord Palmerston, was antipathetic. His brother had lived at Naples for many years, our Minister at a third-rate Court. Now he had come home and died, and, as far as Lord Palmerston's outside life was concerned, there was an end of him.

Early in the Session of 1857 there sprang up a difficulty in China in reference to a small ship which has ever since been known as the lorcha *Arrow*. The *Arrow*, on a charge of piracy, was boarded by certain Chinese from a war junk, and Sir John Bowring, who was our Governor at Hong-Kong, demanded reparation from Commissioner Yeh. Then arose a quarrel and a fight, in which, of course, the English got the better. The matter, which was of importance at the time, has by lapse of years become so trivial as to be hardly worthy of notice here,—but that it led to a dissolution of Parliament. A motion was brought forward in the House of Lords by Lord Derby, blaming the Government, and was carried by a majority of thirty-six. Mr. Cobden brought a similar motion before the House of Commons, and was supported by Mr. Disraeli, Lord John Russell, Sir James Graham, and Mr. Gladstone. Mr. Disraeli twitted Lord Palmerston with having made his complaint to the country, and bade him follow his complaint by an appeal. The motion was carried by a majority of sixteen against the Government, and Lord Palmerston did appeal.

That Lord Palmerston, as Prime Minister, should have been distasteful to Mr. Cobden and Mr. Gladstone we can understand. He was essentially a War Minister, and had latterly dealt with war alone. To Mr. Cobden and Mr. Gladstone he must have been the incarnation of insular aggression. But Lord Derby and Sir James Graham, Lord John Russell and Mr. Disraeli, could have entertained none of this feeling. They had shown themselves at least anxious to conduct the war, and we cannot imagine that the question of the lorcha *Arrow* can have so operated upon them as to make them feel it imperative for the sake of England's glory to turn instantly upon the man who had just brought England through her difficulties. It was simply a party conflict, in which Aristides had been too just. But Aristides resolved that he would follow his enemies' advice, and see what the country would say to it.

He must have known when he went to the country what would be the result. He had just carried the war to a successful end, and the country would not see him displaced. The normal Englishman was thoroughly proud of him, proud of his bad jokes, proud of his unflinching energy, and proud of his years. He called his opponents, when they denied that they combined together against him, "the fortuitous concourse of atoms." The joke was better worth quoting than those he usually made. The country was even proud of him because he stuck to Tiverton instead of accepting a more glorious seat. To have deserted old friends in his glory, who had been true to him before his glory came, would not have been like Palmerston. So he got his majority in spite of the lorcha *Arrow*, and Mr. Bright and Mr. Cobden were both excluded from the new Parliament.

Then came upon us the Indian Mutiny; and men who had never doubted during the Russian campaign, though they felt that England must strain every nerve for victory, began to fear that the few who were there to bear the brunt must perish in the attempt. It was a common fear that if India was to belong to us for the future, India must be conquered a second time; and while men thought of this, their hearts fell within them as they remembered what must be the fate of the British men, and children, and women, who were doomed to suffer things many times worse than death. And there was a feeling by no means uncommon, and very deadly, that India would be lost for ever, and with it all the glory of England. That this idea prevailed in France, which had just been our ally, and in Russia, which had just been our enemy, and in the United States, which of all nations was the nearest akin to us, cannot be doubted. When men's hearts are so heavy they show it in their faces rather than by their speech. There were months in 1857 when men in England hardly dared to speak aloud what they thought and felt about India. But of Lord Palmerston it must be said that he was made of some stronger and coarser fabric than other men, better prepared for hard wear, and able to bear without detriment rain and snow and dirty weather. Through that period of the Indian Mutiny,—which must have been harder, we think, for an English Prime Minister to bear even than the temporary failures of the Crimea,—he never blanched.

It was said by the *Edinburgh Review*, just before the tidings of the Mutiny reached us, that "the past Session found Lord Palmerston covered with the glory of having trodden down the wine-press alone." This was the very pinnacle of the column of praise which was raised to his honour on behalf of his steadfastness against Russia by those of the Press who supported his side in politics. But it was true. He had done it alone. If we look back we can find no other Minister who had not failed, or hesitated, or remained in the background. But yet we think that the effort made by him to suppress the Indian Mutiny was the greater of the two. It came easier to him because he had been made familiar with the efforts necessary for such work by the Russian war; and coming, as the Mutiny did, close after the Russian war, and dealing with matters less palpably open to the mind's eye than the Russian quarrel, it created, with all its horrors and all its triumphs, a less abiding thoughtfulness. India had been ours, and must be ours. So we felt when India was again ours. But it had nearly come to pass that India, at any rate for the time, was not ours. But Palmerston went on governing the country through it all with apparent equanimity. In three months we had sent 30,000 troops to India, with all their horses, appurtenances, clothing, and armour. When we remember the distance, the rapidity required, the scattered positions of the men to be collected, and of the transports needed, I think we may boast that no other country ever made such an effort.

After all, much of the hardest fighting was done by the army stationary in India before the troops from England arrived. It would be unfair to say even a few words about the mutiny without declaring this. Delhi had been taken from the mutineers. Outram, Havelock, the Lawrences, and Inglis had done their work. When all were true and all were heroes, there need be no jealousy of praise. But to Lord Canning, the son of Palmerston's old tutor in politics, the Canning who had been so hard on Palmerston in the Don Pacifico debate, the Canning who had gone to India most unwillingly in obedience to Palmerston's commands, the Canning to have said a word against whom required the self-annihilation of a Minister,[N] Canning who completed by his death his victory in the country he had been sent to govern,—to him and to those brave men whom the Mutiny, bursting from its swarthy ranks, had found in India, the first praise for crushing it is due.

Lord Palmerston in the Mansion House had to blow England's trumpet in addressing the normal Mansion House audience. "An Englishman," he said, "is not so fond as the people of some other countries are of uniforms, of steel scabbards, and of iron heels; but no nation can excel the English, either as officers or soldiers, in knowledge of the duties of the military profession, and in the zeal and ability with which those duties are performed; and whatever desperate deeds are to be accomplished,—wherever superior numbers are to be boldly encountered and triumphantly overcome—wherever privations are to be encountered, wherever that which a soldier has to confront is individually or collectively to be found, there, I will venture to say, there is no nation on the face of the earth which can surpass,—I might, without too much national vanity, say, I believe there is no nation which can equal,—the people of the British islands. But, my Lord Mayor and gentlemen, while we all admire the bravery, the constancy, and the intrepidity of our countrymen in India, we must not forget to do justice also to our countrywomen. In the ordinary course of life the functions of women are to cheer the days of adversity, to soothe the hours of suffering, and to give additional brilliancy to the sunshine of prosperity; but our countrywomen in India have had occasion to show qualities of a higher and nobler kind, and when they have had either to sustain the perils of the siege, or endure the privations of a difficult escape, to forget their own sufferings in endeavouring to minister to the wants of others, the women of the United Kingdom have, wherever they have been found in India, displayed qualities of the noblest kind, such as have never been surpassed in the history of the world. Henceforth the bravest soldier may think it no disparagement to be told that his courage and his power of endurance are equal to those of an Englishwoman."

We can hear the words of the old man now, and tell ourselves that this was a moment in which national vanity might be forgiven. And we can hear the cheers, laden with vanity, as also with true glory, with which they were received. There had been some discussion during the Mutiny as to the expediency of accepting such foreign helps as had been offered. Two Belgian regiments had been suggested. But Lord Palmerston had set his face against all assistance, even from Belgium. He wrote as follows to Lord Clarendon on the matter;—"The more I think of it, the more I feel it is necessary for our standing and reputation in the world that we should put down this mutiny and restore order by our own means; and I am perfectly certain that we can do it, and that we shall do it." And now it had been done.

We must pause for a moment here, to state that a Bill was now brought before Parliament for entirely altering the system under which India was governed. My readers will probably know that up to this time the East India Company did exist, with the power, which had gradually been curtailed indeed, and brought more or less under Government control, of managing the affairs of India as though it were simply the scene of certain commercial transactions. There was a Board of Control attached to the Government, but there was no Secretary of State for India. There was a Board of Directors, but no Indian Council directly appointed by Government. And my readers also know that there is at present a Secretary of State, equal in rank to the other Secretaries; and that India has become a branch of our Government,—as the Colonies are, and Foreign Affairs. I do not know that I need go further into the nature of the change effected than to say that it was carried out in conformity with the proposition made by Lord Palmerston, and in compliance with the Queen's Speech in the previous December. This was done early in 1858. There was a long debate on the first reading, and infinite delays were proposed. This was chiefly due to Mr. Disraeli. He declared that "at present we are undertaking an immense liability; we are entering into engagements which will some day make us tremble; and we have no security whatever that those who really possess power in India, who really manage the resources of the country, will be in the least controlled for our benefit." Nevertheless, upon a division, the Bill was carried by a majority of 145, against an amendment moved, recommending delay. Such was the end of the East India Company as a ruling power; and since that date India has been simply a dependency of the British throne, as are Canada and the Australias. This, too, is to be reckoned among the performances of Lord Palmerston.

Then there arose a question on which Lord Palmerston was most absurdly turned out of office; and he remained out from February, 1858, to June, 1859. It was done absurdly, because the matter in dispute was one in which, not only the country, but also the House of Commons, was altogether at one with him. An attempt had been made to murder the Emperor of the French. It had been done in a manner altogether reckless of human life, the number killed and wounded when the Emperor escaped having been stated as high as 150. And the horror was felt to have been aggravated when it was known that the Empress had been with the Emperor when the attempt was made. Orsini, an Italian, was the leader of the gang by whom the grenades were thrown beneath the Emperor's carriage; and it came out in evidence that Orsini, with his fellow-assassins, had lived in England, and had here constructed his murderous machine. The French Minister of the Emperor applied to our Foreign Office for co-operation in the matter, and desired that the law might be so altered as to make it impossible that suspected assassins,—assassins suspected—should to be so by the English or French Government, be able to carry on their trade in London. Lord Palmerston assented, and a Bill, intending to give the Ministry of the day the power of dealing with such persons, was carried in the House of Commons by a majority of no less than 200. This may be taken as the outspoken opinion of the House, when its feeling was simply one of indignant wrath in regard to Orsini.

But in the meantime the "French Colonels" had signalized themselves. The French Colonels were certain officers who were indignant on the matter. They had known that Orsini had brought his grenades from London, but had not known that the British Government was anxious to do as the French Ministers would have them. They consequently sent various addresses to the Emperor, in which the abominable conduct of England was described in very strong language. The "Colonels" appeared to have thought that all England had been engaged in making murderous weapons for the accommodation of Orsini. And these addresses were unfortunately published in the *Moniteur*, whereby a quasi-official authority was attached to them; because all things published in the *Moniteur* were supposed to have received an official stamp. The French Ambassador expressed his regret, stating that the addresses had passed into the *Moniteur* without notice, and Lord Palmerston urged the House to disregard the vapourings of the "Colonels." But the insult to the nation was there, in the columns of the *Moniteur*, and was much more widely known than the apology which had been sent. There does appear to have been some lack of official despatches which might have been made known to the House. At any rate, an amendment was now proposed,—"That this House cannot but regret that Her Majesty's Government, previously to inviting the House to amend the law of conspiracy at the present time, have not felt it to be their duty to reply to the important despatch received from the French Government, dated January 20"—and this was carried by a majority of 19.

When that former strong expression of opinion had been given by 299 votes to 99, the Government had been supported by the desire of the Tories at large, to keep down such a nest of hornets as Orsini and his conspirators. To banish them from the country, or to hang them if it were necessary, must have seemed good, and did seem good, to Lord Derby's party. And it was not the less good because of the French "Colonels"—who after all were a gallant set of fellows enough, standing up for their country and their Emperor. But it was seen that an instant advantage might be taken of Lord Palmerston and his Government; and they who led the Tory party were not slow to take advantage of it. Lord Palmerston, who seems to have been moved to wrath by such desertion, resigned on the following day, and Lord Derby came into office with Mr. Disraeli as his first lieutenant. Palmerston remained out for sixteen months; but before we go with him into comparative obscurity, we must point out that he had now been dismissed—on the motion too of Mr. Milner Gibson, one of his old enemies, the peace-party,—not because as of yore he was supposed to have been arrogant on the part of England, and in the general course of his policy to have given offence to foreign nations; but because he was supposed,—erroneously supposed,—to have truckled to French orders. Palmerston was the same as ever; but so also was the English nation. When he was accused of arrogance abroad, he was dear old Pam to the normal Englishman. But when he was foolishly conceived to have unduly yielded an inch to French influence, there came instantly to his opponents the power of turning him out,—which his opponents were not slow to do.

During his holiday he took the chair at the Royal Literary Fund dinner, and there, as elsewhere, he made a speech serviceable to the occasion. To make a speech at the Literary Fund dinner seems to be a duty expected from an ex-Prime Minister. Then came a Reform Bill introduced by the Tories;—this was in 1859. But Lord John was not going to accept a Reform Bill from the Tories as long as he could avoid it. The Government was left in a minority, Lord John having moved an amendment condemning the Tory Bill. Thereupon Lord Derby went out, and the Queen was again called upon to form a Ministry.

These formations of new Ministries seem to come very rapidly in the record of one man's life, and to be passed by as though they were matters of no real importance! But to us looking back now over the intervening years,—and twenty-three years have intervened,—how momentous was that unexpected sending for Lord Granville when Lord Derby retired! Lord John Russell and Lord Palmerston had made a compact together that, as the Queen might choose between them, either would help the other; Lord Palmerston had by this time resolved to abandon his wrath, and Lord John, who expected probably to regain his ascendency, still would not decline to serve a second time under his old colleague should the Queen require him. But the claims of the two were equal, and Lord Granville, as being between them, was selected. When Lord Palmerston had before been asked to reconstruct a Ministry, the country had been at war, and every Englishman was in earnest. Then there had been no alternative. But now there could be no reason why Lord Palmerston should not go back to the ranks; though there might be a reason why he should not serve under Lord John. When it was suggested to Lord Palmerston that he should serve under Lord Granville he wrote as follows to the Queen; "Viscount Palmerston and Lord John Russell, before they called the meeting at Willis's Rooms, came to an agreement to co-operate with each other in the formation of a new Administration, whichever of the two might be called upon by your Majesty to reconstruct your Majesty's Government. That agreement did not extend to the case of any third person; but Viscount Palmerston conceives that the same sense of public duty which had led him to enter into that engagement with Lord John Russell should also lead him to give assistance to Lord Granville towards the execution of your Majesty's commands. Viscount Palmerston's promise to Lord Granville has, however, been conditional." "The promise therefore, which he has given to Lord Granville has been made conditional on Lord Granville's success in organizing a Government so composed as to be calculated officially to carry on the public service, and to command the confidence of Parliament and of the country." But Lord Granville was not successful. He found, we are told, that Lord John was unwilling to serve under him, and at the same time to leave the leadership of the House of Commons in Lord Palmerston's hands. Consequently Lord Palmerston was again sent for, and became a second time Prime Minister in his seventy-fifth year.

❑❑❑

CHAPTER XIII

Palmerston as Prime Minister, From 1859 To His Death

THE unification of Italy was the first matter of importance to which Lord Palmerston's new Cabinet had to apply itself. Lord John Russell was Foreign Secretary, but we perceive that Palmerston kept a hold of the reins himself. The things chiefly to be done were as follows. Austria still held Venetia, but had been made to abandon Lombardy by Marshal Mac Mahon at the battle of Magenta. Austria had to be put down and made to depart out of Venetia if possible. France had been victorious; but the Emperor claimed as his reward Savoy and Nice. It was too late for Palmerston to save Savoy and Nice. That blot on poor Cavour's name must remain a stain for ever. He had told our Minister at Turin that they were not to be given up, and had known when he said so that their doom had been spoken. But the Emperor must be stopped and not allowed to run headlong with the *éclat* of his victories. In this matter the Emperor, too, had deceived him. And Italy must be encouraged to take her place among the nations of Europe.

These were the matters as to which, in regard to Italy, the British Cabinet was at the present moment anxious. Palmerston's dislike to Austria,—we might almost call it hatred,—still remained hot as ever. In a memorandum prepared for the Cabinet, Lord Palmerston defended Napoleon as against Austria. "Austria took our subsidies, bound herself by treaty not to make peace without our concurrence, sustained signal defeat in battle, and precipitately made peace without our concurrence. But on what occasion has the Emperor Napoleon so acted?—on none." This was written in January, 1860; but a little later on, when the story of Savoy and Nice was known, he shows his jealousy of Napoleon. In April of the same year, he writes to Lord Cowley at Paris; "The Emperor's mind is as full of schemes as a warren is full of rabbits, and, like rabbits, his schemes go to ground for the moment to avoid notice or antagonism." And there is a record of a conversation which he had with Count Flahault a few days previously. Count Flahault was just going to Paris, and asked him what he should say to the Emperor. The Prime Minister was, what we shall call, very outspoken. England desired peace, he said, but if the Emperor was desirous of war, he would find that England was quite ready for him. And he says in a letter to the Duke of Somerset; "I have watched the Emperor narrowly, and have studied his character and conduct. You may rely upon it, that at the bottom of his heart there rankles a deep and inextinguishable desire to humble and punish England." He says to Lord Cowley; "The seizure of Savoy and Nice, and the breach of promise towards Switzerland about the cession of the Swiss of the neutralized district, are matters which cannot be got over easily." From these quotations it will be seen how intent he was on keeping the Emperor in his place, and saving this country, if it might be saved, from some future battle of Dorking. But in regard to the state of Italy at the time, he had expressed himself very strongly in the memorandum above quoted; "There can be no reasonable doubt, therefore, that both France and Sardinia would unite with England in maintaining the principle that the Italians should be secured against foreign compulsion, and should be left free to determine, according to their own will, what shall be their future political condition."

In all these matters Lord Palmerston and Lord John Russell were, between them, successful—at any rate in the accomplishment of their wishes. Austria was altogether driven out of Italy. The French Emperor did not attempt to avenge Waterloo. And Italy has become a united nation, ruling herself in accordance with her own will.

But in order to make good the boasts which he had made to Count Flahault, it was necessary that the country should be on its guard. Its security, by military means, was always present to Lord Palmerston's mind. He had written a letter in December, 1859, to Mr. Gladstone on the subject, and he must, we should think, have startled Mr. Gladstone by the nonchalant audacity with which he proposed that ten or eleven millions should be at once voted for fortifications to defend Portsmouth and Plymouth. Then he goes into the manner in which the money should be raised,—as to which we cannot but imagine that Mr. Gladstone had his own way. But the millions were voted, and the fortifications were erected; and the Volunteer Force was set on foot,—with what enormous results is now patent to the whole country. In consequence of what was then done, England has now got a double army, one for service abroad, and the other at home. It is only now beginning to be seen and understood that the defence of our own shores may be trusted to men less expensively organized than in regiments of the line.

In 1861 Lord Palmerston was installed as Warden of the Cinque Ports, by which he obtained the use of what was believed to be a comfortable residence near Dover. As Broadlands and Brocket Hall, as well as Cambridge House, in Piccadilly, to which he had long since removed, were all on his hands, this could not have been much to him. But the installation gave him at any rate the pleasure of going down once more to Tiverton, and meeting his old friend Mr. Rowcliffe, the butcher. For the Wardenship was an office, so called, of profit, and the new election was necessary. He was returned without a contest, but not without the usual preliminary discussion with Mr. Rowcliffe.

It is hardly possible to refer to all the measures, or even to all those of importance, with which Lord Palmerston was concerned at this period of his life. In 1860 the paper duties had been discussed; and now that this matter has been well-nigh forgotten among the things that have been quickly settled, we can hardly realize the disturbance to our feelings, and even the animosity, which they created. The House of Lords took upon itself to throw the bill out; whereas a remission of taxation is an affair which the Lower House conceives to belong exclusively to itself. But Palmerston, whose own heart was hardly in the matter, but who was much concerned in keeping peace between the two Houses, contrived to smooth matters down, so that the bill was passed in 1861, and nothing more has been since heard of the paper duties. To us it seems that a penny is, and ever has been, the normal price of a daily newspaper,—unless when the *Times*, or some other daily journal if there be another, chooses on behalf of old gentlemen and ladies to be absurdly luxurious at threepence.

In 1861 the American War of Secession commenced, and in the same year, on the 14th of December, the Prince Consort died. It must have been pleasant to Lord Palmerston to remember that all feelings of animosity,—or rather of hard judgment against him,—had passed away. We can all remember the intense personal sorrow with which the death of the Prince was received by us. A good man had gone from among us, leaving vacant a place which could never more be filled. A man so good at all points is a rare possession, and England has never ceased to want him and to mourn him.

Almost exactly at the same time there sprang up an incident in the American War of Secession which nearly carried us into the whirlpool in spite of the careful efforts we made to avoid the danger. The Southern States had seceded because they had been unwilling to see the government of the country pass from them, the Democratic party, into the hands of their opponents, the Republicans. The Democratic party had grown up and been in power almost since the days of the Adamses, and now felt aware that all their most cherished political institutions were endangered by the appointment of Mr. Lincoln as President. Mr. Lincoln was a thorough Republican. To show how the two parties had hitherto fought the battle, each by the creation of new States which should, or should not, foster slavery within their boundaries, is too long a task to be undertaken here. Should Texas, which was devoted to slavery, become one State or should it be four? Should Kansas be slave or free? Should Nevada and Nebraska, free-soil States as they would be, be admitted or excluded? Each State must have two Senators, and on the number of Senators the manipulation of the powers of government depended. The growing wealth and population of the North at last won the day, and the South, seeing how it was with them, determined to secede. They did endeavour to secede, and a state of war was the consequence.

There can now be no doubt, I think, in any unprejudiced mind that the sole effort made by the English Government during the war was to hold their own hands with absolute impartiality, and allow the Americans to fight it out. In private life, opinions varied; and, following a broad line, we may say that the commercial classes were in favour of the North, and the agricultural and the aristocratic of the South. And these feelings, either on the one side or the other, were enhanced by the growing deficiency of cotton. We find even Lord Palmerston suggesting that the idea of a French Ambassador should be entertained, for compelling the Northern States to let cotton from the South make its way to Europe. A more unjust, or indeed impossible, solution of the difficulty could not be found. But Palmerston simply mentioned the matter to a colleague in the Cabinet, and the question of interference or non-interference, of recognition or the reverse, was, as far as outsiders could perceive, left chiefly in the hands of Lord Russell, who was Foreign Secretary. Lord John had been created a peer in July, 1861. By the entire Cabinet the decision was come to that England would not interfere, and would not recognize the South. As far as the English Government was concerned, of which Lord Palmerston was the head, such was its line of policy from first to last; and the Northern party in the war was certainly not justified in feeling animosity against England.

But such a feeling was very strong in the States. It was thought that England should at once have patted the North on the back, as having that side in the quarrel to which manifest justice belonged. Then sprang up the *Trent* affair, which, but for the united wisdom of two men in the States, of Mr. Lincoln and Mr. Seward his Chief Secretary, would certainly have brought us into war. And here, no doubt, Lord Palmerston did take an active part in preparing, under certain circumstances, for active measures.

As the North believed in England's enmity, so did the South in her friendship. As the fighting became brisk and hard, could they not send two Commissioners to England to arrange terms for their recognition? With this view Messrs. Slidell and Mason were to be sent. But passenger ships did not run then from Charleston to Liverpool with more freedom than cotton ships. The gentlemen had to be smuggled to England, and made their way as far as Cuba on their road. One would say that the difficulties of the journey were then overcome. And so they thought when they took their places on board the British mail steamer *Trent,* which ran from the Havanah to St. Thomas. At St. Thomas they would be as though they were in England.

But there is many a slip betwixt the cup and the lip. As the *Trent* was running up to St. Thomas, she was stopped by an American man-of-war, the *San Jacinto*, under the command of the redoubtable Captain Wilkes, and the Southerners were taken out of her and carried back to Boston. A great fuss was made about the achievement, as though Captain Wilkes had done something very heroic, and there was some talk of giving him a sword. Thanks were voted to him by Congress. He had done nothing but a policeman's work, and had done it without orders. But it was conceived he had gone halfway to beating the South,—and not only the South, but England also.

It was then that the Guards were sent to Canada. It was the quickly expressed determination of England, in uttering which Lord Palmerston was the mouthpiece of the country, that unless these two men were sent over to England at once,—or were enabled to make the journey which they had promised themselves when they got on board the *Trent,*—our Minister should be withdrawn, and war should be declared. A man-of-war did come to the Potomac, ready to take away Lord Lyons and his suite. In Washington, we heard that on the next day war was to have been declared,—unless Mr. Lincoln and Mr. Seward yielded. Mr. Sumner, who as Chairman of the Committee of the Senate on Foreign Politics was something akin to our Foreign Secretary, was hot against it. He was supposed to be the true patriotic American of the day. But before we went to bed that night in Washington we had been told that Messrs. Slidell and Mason were to be sent on to England. When they got there they could do nothing for the recognition of the

South. England passed through that danger, and Lord Palmerston was enabled to think of other things.

We are drawing now to the end of Lord Palmerston's career, and have only further to notice the Schleswig-Holstein affair, and the great debate which took place respecting it in July, 1864. There had previously been questions of the ill-treatment of the Poles by Russia, and of the re-modelling of the Treaty of Vienna. In neither of these matters was anything effectual done by England; but in both of them Palmerston showed the caution which had come to him, not from years, but from his thorough acquaintance with the state of Europe. England had seen the third Napoleon become, as it were, her natural ally. But against the craft of the Emperor our Prime Minister was specially on his guard. France desired confirmation for what had lately passed, and a new Treaty, so that Europe should be re-arranged as she specially desired to arrange it; and France specially wanted some plea by which she could stretch her boundaries as far as the Rhine. This matter is only interesting to us now as showing the care which Lord Palmerston, on the part of England, exercised in his latter days against his old friend the Emperor.

Then came the affair of Schleswig-Holstein, which it would be very difficult to explain in the penultimate chapter of such a book as this; and which would be very uninteresting if explained. Denmark was undoubtedly Denmark. Holstein was undoubtedly German, though at present she was under the dominion of the King of Denmark. Schleswig may be said to have been half one and half the other. The encroachments of Prussia, destined to envelop all adjacent German-speaking countries, had commenced; and Austria, having then a part in the German Diet, joined herself with Prussia in attacking Denmark. Here, in England, the general opinion was undoubtedly in favour of Denmark. It was so in the British interpretation of the law of Europe on the subject; and also in the idea that a little country was undergoing ill-usage from two others that were much larger and more powerful. Lord Russell, as Foreign Secretary, became indignant, and said words which enabled his eager friends and his active enemies to declare that he had promised assistance to Denmark. Lord Palmerston, always since the days of Savoy and Nice on his guard against the Emperor of the French, and having, as Prime Minister, reversed his character as the general tyrant of Europe, wrote as follows to his colleague: "I share fully your indignation. The conduct of Austria and Prussia is discreditably bad, and one, or both of them, will suffer for it before these matters are settled. I rather doubt, however, the expediency of taking at the present moment the steps proposed. The French Government would probably decline it, unless tempted by the suggestion that they should place an armed force on the Rhenish frontier in the event of a refusal by Austria and Prussia,—which refusal we ought to reckon as nearly certain." But he partially agreed with Lord Russell. He wrote to the Duke of Somerset; "I own I quite agree with Russell, that our squadron ought to go to Copenhagen as soon as the season will permit, and that it ought to have orders to prevent any invasion of, or attack upon, Zealand and Copenhagen."

Louis Napoleon at last refused to join with us in any attempt to be made on behalf of the Danes. He saw no reason for fighting with the Germans unless he were to be allowed to stretch himself to the Rhine. Lord Russell,—and with him the British Cabinet,—found himself unable to undertake the task single-handed; and consequently Denmark was abandoned, and the Government had to bear the reproach of having deserted their friend. An attack was made upon it in both Houses. In the House of Lords, Lord Palmerston and his colleagues were beaten by a majority of nine; and Mr. Disraeli brought the matter forward in the Commons with many thunderclaps of furious speech. He asked the House to agree with him that the Government "had lowered the just influence of their country in the councils of Europe, and thereby destroyed the securities for peace." The debate lasted for four nights, and Mr. Disraeli's thunderclap of elocution was certainly loud and frightful. To tell the truth his speech on the occasion was very strong. Lord Palmerston spoke on the last day; and as he went down to the House, day after day, all the people cheered him. There was at the moment a feeling against Lord Russell, because it was thought that he had promised the Danes much, and had performed little. But Palmerston was still the people's favourite, and they cheered him to the last. He altogether laid aside the matter at issue, and went into the general question of the merits of the Government. Let the people of the country see what had been done by the present Government for the taxes of the country, and then he would be afraid of no vote which the House of Commons could give against him. The Government got a majority of eighteen, and were thus re-established in power, at any rate till the next session.

This had taken place in 1864, and the speech he had then delivered was the last of the great efforts he had made on that arena. During the next year he reached his eightieth birthday. In that same year Parliament, having nearly run out its term of existence, was dissolved, and he was again elected for Tiverton. He went from thence to Brocket Hall, having chosen that residence because of its vicinity to London, and there, with Lady Palmerston to watch over him, he breathed his last. It is a singular fact that in the room adjacent to that in which he died another Prime Minister of England had left this troublesome world but a few years previously, and Lady Palmerston had been the sister of that other Prime Minister.

They laid him in Westminster, among the statesmen and men of letters of whom his country was proud, and they put up a statue to his name in the close neighbourhood of the Chamber in which he had sat almost continuously since it had been built thirty years before. What more could they do to perpetuate his memory? But all that would have been nothing had he not made for himself a lasting position in the minds of Englishmen.

Looking back through all the History of England and her worthies, I do not know the life of any man who has shown such a career of unchequered good fortune and jocund happiness,—or more unblemished honesty and truer courage.

❑❑❑

CHAPTER XIV

Conclusion

PALMERSTON'S great merit as a governing man arose from his perfect sympathy with those whom he was called upon to govern;—and his demerit, such as it was, sprang from the same cause. He was bold, industrious, honest, strong in purpose as in health, eager, unselfish, and a good comrade. He was at the same time self-asserting, exacting, never doubting himself when his opinion had been formed, and confident against the world in arms. We cannot be surprised that such a one should have been loved by us, and still less so that he should have been hated by others. He was an enemy to the Ministers of other Courts, not only because he was bold, honest, and eager, but also because he showed himself plainly to have those qualities, and was never tired of asserting himself because of them. Who is this man that claims to himself to be more hardworking and honester than any among us,—and who is making good his pretensions? Such were not the spoken words of any foreign statesman of the day; but they describe the feelings on which they seem to have acted. And these men at the same time did believe themselves, and truly believed themselves, to be intellectually his superiors. Let us take Guizot as one of the number, who had much to do with Palmerston, and with whom Palmerston was much concerned. Guizot must have been conscious of brighter faculties and greater thinking power. But he must have been aware that in all discussions among men of the same class Palmerston's word was the strongest, because of his probity, and truth, and industry.

The same idea occurs to us in reading what has been written of him since his death. He is called "stupid" and "blundering" by those who have been opposed to his politics as a War Minister. But such as his politics were, they were always those of his countrymen for the time being; and in a country professing to be ruled under the Constitution which here prevails, I do not know what higher praise can be given to a Minister. Let the people change their principles; let the Cobdens and Brights teach them that war is altogether a bad thing, and that commerce will suffice to procure for us the respect of other nations. I do not say that it may not be so, and that the teaching of Cobden and Bright may not approve itself in the long run. But such has not yet become the opinion of Englishmen generally; and until Cobden and Bright have taught their countrymen, the country requires such a Minister as was Lord Palmerston. They liked his honesty; they liked his self-assertion, and they did not like it the less, because he expressed himself with a hectoring tongue.

Mr. Morley, in his "Life of Cobden," vol. ii. p. 189, has said of Palmerston, that Sir John Bowring was wrong in the affair of the *Arrow*, and should have been recalled. He then goes on as follows; "It was not, however, to be expected from the statesman, whose politics never got beyond *Civis Romanus*, especially when he was dealing with a very weak power." The charge here made is manifestly unjust. Had he said that Palmerston had preached the doctrine of *Civis Romanus* against all nations, weak or strong,—*usque ad nauseam*,—there might have been some truth in the saying. But the sting of the reproach lies in the assertion that he had preached it especially when the weak were opposed to him. He has intended to imply that when Greece or Portugal were concerned, then, on behalf of Britons, Palmerston exclaimed, *Civis Romanus*; but that he lowered his colours and bated his breath when he had to deal with France or Austria, with Russia or Prussia. Against this I protest. Take all the matters in which he was engaged with other countries,—the creation of Belgium, the Spanish marriages, his treatment of Metternich and Buol, and his life-long battle with Nicholas, and then say whether he was *Civis Romanus* "especially with the weaker powers!" The word has escaped Mr. Morley in the pride of his contempt, and should be recalled from a work destined to live long because of merits which his prejudice cannot obscure.

But we do know that Lord Palmerston was unpopular among the foreigners, especially in the early part of his career. Mr. Greville thus wrote of him in his journal in 1834; "Madame de Lieven told me that it was impossible to describe the contempt as well as dislike which the whole *corps-diplomatique* had for Palmerston, and, pointing to Talleyrand, who was sitting close by, 'surtout lui.' They have the meanest opinion of his capacity, and his manners are the reverse of conciliatory." Again, he says, in 1835; "Palmerston is beaten in Hants, at which everyone rejoices." But by degrees Mr. Greville mends his verdict. "The other night I met some clerks in the Foreign Office to whom the very name of Palmerston is hateful. But I was surprised to hear them,—Mellish particularly, who can judge both from capacity and opportunity,—give ample testimony to his abilities."

It will be seen from this that even among Englishmen likely to be intimate with the diplomatic circle in London, so late as 1835 Lord Palmerston was supposed to have been generally unpopular, and his want of punctuality is spoken of, a fault likely to interfere much with the comfort of others. But at that time he was a man of fashion, and though he had been for many years specially noted for his industry in mastering all the details of his office,—at the War Office for instance, through his many years of service before he was appointed to the Foreign Office,—it may be surmised that he preferred to work at such hours as best suited himself. If this was so, it only gives an additional proof of that determination to have his own way which governed him through all his life. But his popularity as a Minister did not commence even among Englishmen till after the dates above quoted from Mr. Greville's journal;—nor that respect among foreigners, did in fact mean a reverence for the power he exercised. It was not in truth known to the world at large how great had been his influence in regard to the creation of Belgium, nor how powerful had been his policy as to the quadruple alliance, till long after the period in question. And though he was sowing the seed for that respect which afterwards grew till he had become the arbiter of European politics generally, the men in whose minds the seed was growing would not, to themselves, admit the growth until the full plant was there, ripe for the use of the nations. In such a career it was necessary that the man should be hated before he was esteemed. Therefore it was that Madame de Lieven spoke of him with contempt, and told of him how Talleyrand specially disliked him. Had he been courteous and servile, and fit to take a place among themselves, the Russian lady and the French gentlemen would have loved the polished man of fashion well enough.

And in those days Palmerston was a Tory, though he was a member of a Whig Government. It must be remembered that the death of Mr. Pitt was still nearer than the death of Lord Palmerston himself. There had to run more than thirty years before the latter event came. It was less than thirty years since Pitt had died. And Palmerston was still regarded as a man brought up in the courtly manner; and the fashion after which he was prepared to form a way of living for himself was not yet deciphered or understood. It was not believed that he intended to be so wise, so plastic, and so attentive a politician. In this respect he was running the same career which Canning had taken before him, and which Gladstone has taken since;—and which indeed Peel may be said to have adopted in the last year or two of his life. He had grown into accord with the people of whom he was one. But neither did he do this as Canning had done, with whom it was an affair of genius, of impulse, and of anger; nor as Peel, with whom it was conscience; nor as Gladstone, on whose versatile mind all motives which are not ignoble seemed to have acted with dangerous rapidity. Palmerston changed slowly without knowing that he changed, and learned to wear the common garb of an Englishman because Englishmen around him wore it. "It is a brave spectacle," says the *Edinburgh*, in an eloquent article on his death, written in January, 1866;—"it is a brave spectacle to look back on, to see the skill and courage with which nearly single-handed he fought and baffled continental despotism for more than thirty years." "Since Cromwell's time no other British statesman has had the honour of having his name made a bugbear to frighten children and despot-ridden lands." "He was accused of being insolent and aggressive; he was accused of being truckling and cowardly. But now that he is gone there is not a man of us but would say, with his generous antagonist, 'We are all proud of him,'" The generous antagonist had been Sir Robert Peel; and the words he then spoke were the last which he uttered in the House of Commons. The writer then goes on;—"He is gone; peace to his ashes! It is sad to think we shall never see again that pleasant face, that jaunty air, still dashed by a tinge of the dandyism of the regency, that never-failing figure on the Treasury Bench which drew all eyes; never hear the cheery trumpet tone, not unmusical in its cadences; never learn from his graver wisdom, nor meet his old familiar smile again. We laid him in Westminster Abbey with pride as well as sorrow, side by side with the dust of his great compeers, not dearer or mightier than he. He was a great man. He loved his country and his country loved him. He lived for her honour, and she will cherish his memory."

As I am now quoting what was said of him shortly after his death, I will give an extract from an article which appeared in August, 1868, in the *Saint Paul's Magazine*, and was from the hand of Mr. Peter Bayne;—

"When we were at war with Russia, and when the nation, after trying statesman after statesman, continued in the distressing consciousness that the administration lacked vigour, the man who, for a quarter of a century, had been checkmating the policy of Russia was naturally called for. In no spirit of confidence or enthusiasm,—feeling clearly that others had failed, but by no means certain that the right man was yet discovered,—England said, 'Try Palmerston.' It was on the 8th of February, 1855, that the Earl of Derby withdrew, and that he took the helm. On the 16th he explained his position to the House. Already all the machinery of an energetic administration was at work, and as the new Prime Minister glanced at department after department, detailing what had been done and what was planned, members felt that a new spirit of energy was already penetrating the framework of Government. The country looked on in hope, beginning to breathe more freely. Month after month went by; month after month the public watched. Troubles came at first in threatening battalions upon the Ministry; but the practical instinct of the nation gradually decided that Palmerston was the man to whom the business of the war could be committed, and in whose hands the name of England was safe. It was astonishing with what ease he held the reins at that noisy time, and with what lightness and self-possession he encountered the obstacles in his path. In May the Opposition made a determined attempt to unseat him, and a long and stormy debate took place. Mr. Disraeli, anxious to avail himself of the uneasy and disconted feeling which still widely prevailed, and to make the most of the inarticulate shouting of a number of ill-informed people who called themselves Administrative Reformers, moved a resolution to the effect that the language of Her Majesty's Government was 'ambiguous and uncertain.' The Opposition maintained the attack with spirit and animosity, and the men below the gangway on the Liberal side, in whose eyes Lord Palmerston never found favour, kept up a raking fire of argument, taunt and invective. Mr. Disraeli closed the attack in one of his most impassioned philippics. One can still see him with the mind's eye as his sentences rang through the House, his right arm coming down with fierce emphasis at each rhetorical close, while he asked, in impetuous torrent of interrogatives, whether the Prime Minister had not done this, that, and the other evil thing? It was beautiful to observe Lord Palmerston sitting in fixed and placid attention, cool as an old admiral cut out of oak, the figure-head of a seventy-four gun ship in a Biscay squall. At last, as the hours of morning stole on, he placed his hat quietly on the table, and, amid the intense excitement of the House, sprang to his feet. Not a shade of agitation or anxiety could you trace on that brave, clear, splendidly intelligent face. The forehead, broad and expansive, the eye frank, fearless, and sparkling, the whole countenance radiant with energy, courage, good temper, spoke assurance to his party and defiance to the Opposition. He had got into the heart of his subject,—eleven and a half columns of Hansard had been spoken,—when the cry of 'Black Rod' echoed through the House, and the usher who rejoices in that mysterious title summoned the Commons to the bar of the Lords, to receive her Majesty's assent by commission to certain Bills. Lord Palmerston was interrupted; the Speaker left the chair, and, with as many of the members as chose to accompany him, proceeded to the Upper House. After a while the Speaker returned, and Lord Palmerston resumed. 'I think,'—these were his first words,—'I have some reason to complain of the impatience of the other House in not waiting for the censure which the right honourable gentleman opposite is desirous of inflicting, but in prematurely administering the rod.' The Opposition, joining in the titter which ran along every bench, learned that the tempest they had so passionately raised had agitated the mind of Lord Palmerston to no greater extent than was consistent with its wafting towards them a jest so feather-light as this. The next second he was grappling with the arguments of his opponents, and in one or two minutes all recollection of the interruption had passed from the memory of the House. His speech may be pronounced one of the noblest ever uttered in Parliament. Simple, manly, luminous, convincing, high in tone and unanswerable in reasoning, it told upon the intellect not only of Parliament, not only of England, but of the civilized world. Some of its sentences deserve to be remembered. 'I feel that, in whatever hands the Government is placed, the will of the country must and will be obeyed. I know that will is that England, having engaged in a war necessary and just, in concert with our great ally and neighbour, France, must and shall succeed.' From the moment he was Prime Minister, Lord Palmerston felt that he held a trust higher than the interests of party, and not in the utmost fervour of debate, not in the most unguarded moment of social converse, could an expression pass his lips which, in discrediting his adversaries, cast a slur upon the name of England. In a still loftier tone, one seldom assumed by Lord Palmerston, and never except in a spirit of deep reverence and sincerity, is the following: 'The fate of battle is in the hands of a Higher Power. It is not in our power to command success, but it is enough for us to do all in our power to obtain it. That we have done. In a cause which we consider to be just, necessary, and honourable, we confidently place our trust in a Higher Power.' Mr. Disraeli was beaten by a majority of one hundred, and the Government confirmed in the hands of Lord Palmerston.

"From that night he was a kind of monarch in England. We learned to call him Old Pam, and to love him better than any Prime Minister was ever loved throughout the three kingdoms. All parties in the House took to him. It was pleasant to sit under his parliamentary government, and though there were Liberals more liberal than he, and Conservatives more conservative, the majority both of Liberals and Conservatives secretly preferred him to their special chiefs. He had not the slowness and heavy decorum of Earl Russell; he did not startle country gentlemen with extravagances, paradoxes, and freaks of intellectual rope-dancing, like Mr. Disraeli; and his virtue was not of that grim and earnest kind which rebukes a worldly-minded legislature in the person of Mr. Gladstone. The great neutral party in and out of the House discovered that the firebrand Palmerston would not kindle dangerous conflagrations, but was opulent in the heat that warms without burning."

And further on he says;—

"Perhaps no single word goes so far in the description of Lord Palmerston as the word 'manly.' The feminine element is strong in some men,—they are vehement, impulsive, meekly obstinate, prone to extremes, apt to call whims principles, breaking down all fences of logic in their teacup storms of feeling. In every respect Lord Palmerston was masculine, not feminine. In one of those wise, well-packed bits which you meet with in the writings of Goethe, it is observed that the key to the female character, as distinguished from that of the man, is found in a reference to the personal and private nature of the interests of women as contrasted with the wider interests of men. Her husband, her children, her household,—these are a woman's own, and within the circle of these Nature has ordained that her affections shall have their heartfelt play. These interests are essentially disjunctive; they pertain to the woman alone, and they isolate, while they intensify, her sympathies. The gregariousness of humankind, on the other hand, comes out where man acts in association with man; and man's institution is not the family circle, but the nation. The masculine interests are common to the race, and the mental operation of the man is the impersonal reason which knows no prepossession and rejects all colouring of emotion. The Duke of Wellington occurs to one as specially illustrating Goethe's conception of the masculine mind; and Lord Palmerston was at all points a man. No sentimental egotism, no moral irritability, no sweet feminine cant about him. A genial stoicism,—not the stoicism of the cynic,—an inestimable faculty of taking the good and leaving the bad alone, an invincible serenity and lightness and brightness of soul, distinguished him. Hopeful in adversity, cool in prosperity, ready for any fate, Horace would have smiled approval on him, and mildly exclaimed, 'Bene preparatum pectus!'"

The question has often been mooted whether he was or was not an orator. Before that question be answered, the man who asks it must decide what it is to be an orator. An orator such as Bright and Gladstone, or even as were Disraeli and Lord Derby, as were in former days Mr. Fox, Mr. Burke, or Mr. Pitt, he certainly was not. He would not, like some of these men, have arranged his words with studious care, and have committed the chosen gems of them to his memory; nor, as others have done, could he have burst out under the inspiration of genius into a sudden flow of words to which no study and no memory could have lent anything. To him it seems that oratory was an evil only to be encountered for the sake of certain purposes which could not be otherwise attained. How shall men know a fact unless they be told? Or how shall a man tell a fact so as to induce belief unless he be instructed in the way of doing so? Such was Lord Palmerston's oratory. In the longest, and most telling speeches which he made, he seems never to have thought of the reflex effect upon himself. In his great effort on the Don Pacifico impeachment, or in his reply to Mr. Disraeli in the attack made on Lord Russell in regard to Denmark, his object was to leave such an impression on men's minds that they should ultimately be brought to show their agreement with his side of the question by the votes which they were to give. It was for this reason that he did his best, and not that he might achieve for himself any palm of oratory. Gladstone bursts into speech that the brightness and splendour and marvel of the moment may be his own. Bright is enabled by his intellect and study, and industry, to carry his admiring hearers along with him. In both cases there seems to be left on the hearer's mind a feeling that the orator has without doubt established his right to the name. In the latter there is the sense, perhaps, of too great an expenditure of oil in avoiding a superfluous word. With the other, words run riot with such glorious fecundity as to leave an impression that some oil might have been expended in pruning their abundance. In Palmerston there was neither the one nor the other; but in producing the effect which he generally did achieve, there was always an idea present to the hearer, first, that he did not know exactly the words which would best suit his purpose, and then a feeling that he had fallen into their use by some celestial and godlike aid. It was not Palmerston who had made the speech, but some goddess Fortune who had put the words on to his lips.

By Lord Palmerston his capacity for speaking was only a means used for an end. The same may be said of all orators. To persuade others is the art to be achieved. But this is done in most cases by teaching an audience, or teaching the country to believe that the speaker should be credited with the power he seeks to gain because he is great as an orator. It was not simply because Fox was wise that men ranged themselves on his side; but because from his tongue words flowed sweeter than honey. But with Palmerston there was no thought of words flowing sweet. He had come to a special crisis of some difficulty, and men had to be made to vote as he wished them. When that was done, the speech and all belonging to it was, for his purposes, a thing of the past. He thought not at all that men should be rapt in wonder at his words. But the thing that he was doing, the attempt that he was making, the lesson that he was teaching,—the lesson, for instance, that Palmerston was in truth the man in Europe who best understood how Europe might be governed,—that was his object in view, with as little of speech as might be possible, but still with a sufficiency, as such is the mode of governing in England.

But other means were wanting before any credence could be given to the immense claim he made on the confidence of those of his own country and of others. He had to show that he had learned the lesson he attempted to teach, and could do this only by daily industry and indomitable perseverance. And it must be understood that the industry and the perseverance had come before his ambition had formed itself in reference to the management of Europe. We must go back to his early days, when, after spending two years at the Admiralty, he had been, still a lad, transferred to the War Office, to perceive how resolutely he had begun the work of his life. England was at war, and he determined at once to learn all the ways and all the needs of a warfaring nation. But our wars brought us among foreign people;—to Spain, to Portugal, to France, and to the Low Countries. And in this way Palmerston achieved his knowledge of what they wanted and of what we wanted. He had begun to see the claims of other diplomats, and to contest them before he had won his place at our own Foreign Office. He had been a young man of fashion; but that had been added on, out of the superabundance of his nature. Hard work was to him the first necessity of his existence. He loved to be brilliant at Almack's, but he did not care to carry his brilliance into the House of Commons. It followed him there in his latter years; but that too came from the superabundance of his nature. Some one has said that Palmerston, when at his greatest, was powerful and imperious only with a pen in his hand. We feel that this was so. But it is thus that the official work of a man in office should be done. And as he wrote the scathing letters to his own ambassadors which were intended to be read for the keeping in order of Foreign Ministers, we feel that he was very great. In the course of time they became too bitter. The arbiter of the politics of Europe became like other arbiters, its bully. They who shall hereafter be desirous of saying severe words against him, must if they desire their words to be effectual, confine themselves to this charge. Against his honesty, his industry and his courage we feel that no true word can be said.

❑❑❑

Notes:

A. When quotations from letters or speeches are made in the following pages they are taken from his work, unless it is otherwise stated.

B. "Life of the Prince Consort," vol. ii. p. 419.

C. "Life of the Prince Consort," vol. iii. p. 206.

D. Ibid., vol. ii. p. 275.

E. See the *Edinburgh Review* for January, 1874, p. 196.

F. Morley's "Life of Cobden," vol. i. note on p. 82.

G. "Memoir of Right Hon. John Charles Herries," by his son, Edward Herries, C.B.; with an introduction by Sir Charles Herries, K.C.B.; published 1880.

H. When we read Mr. Kinglake's picturesque account of the manner in which the *Coup d'Etat* was prepared, we find it hard to understand that Lord Palmerston should have believed as he did. It is odd that two honest men should have entertained opinions so different. Lord Palmerston, no doubt, spoke immediately after the event, and the historian did not give his account till ten years later. But in the meantime the Emperor had been generally "approved of" in England, and the question arises whether the approval had been deserved. There were many here in England who never thought so, and to them the assent of Lord Palmerston has always been distressing.

I. I think it should be remembered,—though I cannot give absolute proof for such an opinion,—that Palmerston, previous to the *Coup d'Etat*, had expressed his opinion in favour of an Empire for France; and it is probable that this opinion had previously reached Napoleon's ears. Guided by what he had seen of a former Republic, he did not believe in a new Republic for France. There might have been an idea, on the part of the Crown, that in expressing this opinion, even in private speech or in public writing, he had gone too far. His personal feeling for the Emperor was, no doubt, friendly and strong, till subsequently Nice and Savoy had, as he felt treacherously, been taken from Italy and added to France. At that date Palmerston's personal friendship for the Emperor is supposed to have ceased.

J. The words were;—"If you should be of opinion that recent legislation, in contributing, with other causes, to this happy result, has at the same time inflicted unavoidable injury on certain important interests, I recommend you dispassionately to consider how it may be practicable equitably to mitigate that injury, and to enable the industry of the country to meet successfully that unrestricted competition to which Parliament, in its wisdom, has decided that it should be subjected."

K. "Life of Prince Consort," vol. ii. p. 525.

L. "Invasion of the Crimea," vol. i. p. 374.

M. "Invasion of the Crimea," vol. i. p. 378.

N. Lord Ellenborough, when he was Secretary for India, had found fault with Lord Canning, and had been forced to resign.

❑❑❑